Pork & Sons

Photographs
Marie-Pierre Morel

Illustrations
José Reis de Matos

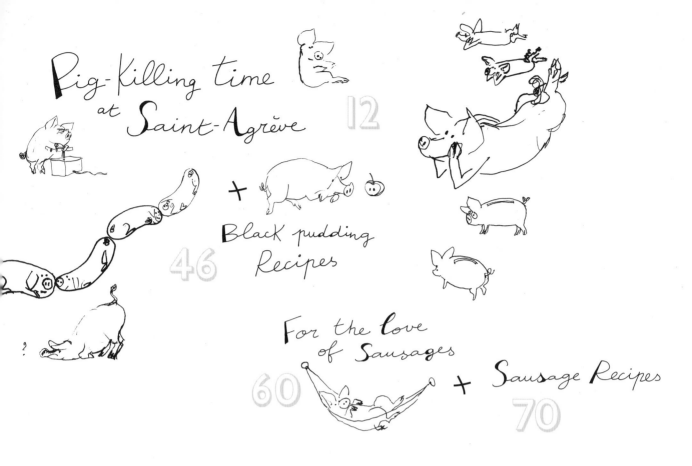

PORK À LA CARTE

4   Contents

granny pig

Barbecued Pork

A piggy party

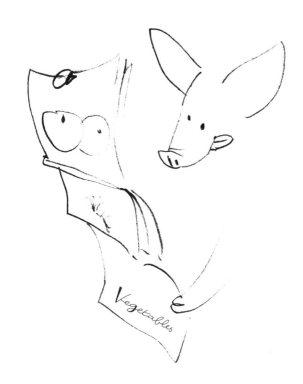

Vegetables

Wild boar

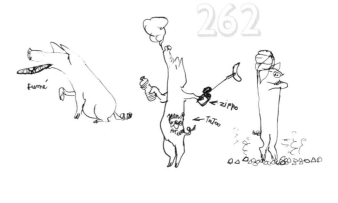

Pépé Barbe

MY GRANDFATHER FRANÇOIS BARBE, KNOWN AS 'MILLEZON'

For over 40 years he presided over the village square as butcher – or rather as professor of butchery! Grandpa knew all about animals. Cattle, calves, lambs, pigs: they were his daily life from Monday through to Sunday. Grandpa was on duty summer and winter, eight days a week. He didn't take many holidays, having a tendency to develop allergies the moment he left Saint-Agrève. He missed its good fresh air! But even if he was somewhat unimaginative in his excuses for not leaving his native village even for a few days, he was easily forgiven. Grandpa worked hard and hard workers earn respect.

At the height of the season it took some effort to get up in the morning when you wouldn't be going to bed again until the next day. For Grandpa rose early, very early. He often told me off, in his own typical way, for vainly trying to lie in now and then, and would regularly – and mischievously – charge into my bedroom about seven in the morning, his apron already showing signs of wear, to wake me up. 'Seven o'clock, Stéphane. You can sleep for another two hours!' Thanks very much, Grandpa, for keeping me so well informed about the progress of the clock! But it was summer, and he had to make butter. If you get up after sunrise the butter just won't 'come'. Malicious tongues, undoubtedly envious of the wonderful weather in Saint-Agrève, will tell you that summer there lasts only from 14 to 15 August, but I have to protest. Let me assure you that summer in Saint-Agrève lasts at least from 10 to 15 August.

In his shop Grandpa, who knew everything about animals, would smile gently at the sight of the summer tourists in their lightweight clothes (only between 10 and 15 August, of course). He was always generous when weighing meat, but somehow managed to sell customers a slicing sausage, a leg of lamb and six quails when all they'd come in to buy was two slices of lean ham! 'English spoken here, *se habla español*' – no language barrier bothered Grandpa when it came to selling his goods. He had even mastered Barbanto – a version of Esperanto spoken by Grandpa Barbe which no one else understood. My Grandpa was a superb businessman.

In winter, it was quite a sight to see Grandpa braving the snowdrifts in search of the best ox liver, the fattest pig, or young calves for veal. At the wheel of his van, head lowered, cap pulled well down, he was a veritable snow-plough, facing the cold wind of the high plateaux on his way to isolated farms. None of the local council road-workers could compete with him. Once he had reached a farm he had to drink a toast; business can't be done without a glass of wine. However, Grandpa was very fastidious. Drinking from a glass that wasn't crystal clear or bore traces of a previous visitor really made him suffer. Everyone knew that and deliberately

Before you read on . . .

Pork & Sons

teased him. People enjoyed watching Grandpa's mouth twist as he took a deep breath before lifting a dirty glass to his lips. Once the wine had been drunk though, business could begin. Grandpa was worth watching as he chose an animal, a gloomy expression on his face, always finding some fault with it before discussing the price – in old francs, and paying in old francs too. (Francs and then new francs were French currency before the introduction of the euro.) Heaven knows how often the bank manager tried explaining that 1 franc and 100 francs were not the same sum of money, and that writing a cheque for 100,000 francs when he was paying for a pig worth 1,000 francs was a sure-fire way to make a lot of farmers very rich. On the other hand, when Grandpa offered me 50 francs for an afternoon's work helping him out, my undernourished money-box – a piggy-bank, of course – ended up with only a miserable 5 centimes.

Grandpa didn't take his secrets with him when he retired. He passed on all his butcher's lore to his son René, the worthy inheritor of the Barbanto language. Taking over the shop from a character like Grandpa gave my uncle a lot of trouble. Grandpa in retirement was much more tiresome than Grandpa at work, for he didn't go away quietly to enjoy spending the money he had worked hard for, not he. The butcher's trade was his whole life, and right to the end he could be found somewhere in the shop, criticizing all kinds of things – new techniques, new rules and regulations – shaking hands with anyone available and repeating, at frequent intervals: 'But what will people say if I'm not here?'

Pigs are no longer slaughtered at the back of the shop ... all that has changed today. The sight of pigs parked in the back yard waiting for the fateful moment to deliver up their carcasses is a thing of the past. Modern standards of hygiene mean that animals can no longer be slaughtered on the premises. The theory and practice of butchery in the good old Barbe fashion lost their original savour, and all of a sudden a child no longer had the opportunity to make a pet of a suckling pig and save it from its destiny – although the fact is that once the pet owner's back was turned, the piglet's fate was sealed. But waste not, want not, as they say. An animal is an animal and we don't shed tears over its fate. Although there was my guinea pig Zouzou, a cute little thing, always snuggling up to something nice and soft in my bedroom. February came and with it the school holidays ... Zouzou went to stay with Grandpa and was found frozen to death in a rabbit hutch at -15 °C (5 °F). It was risky for any animal to come near the Barbe butcher's shop, so much so that when a cat went missing in the village Grandpa was the prime suspect. For the record, the real guilty party was Toupie, a rather vampish alley cat who didn't know the meaning of the word modesty and collected lovers all over the place. She had taken up residence in the loft above the shop, so the local toms all went there for a good night out.

Before you read on . . .

✳

Eventually, Grandpa went to chew the fat with the angels and I'm sure he was relieved to find that no one would make him follow the Catholic tradition of eating only fish on Fridays. Fish on Grandpa's plate was like closing the shop on Sunday – unheard-of. Once Grandpa was gone, René flung himself into his job, heart and soul. Every kind of sausage and other charcuterie went on appearing in the window to tempt all who appreciate good food. So much so that you could hardly pass the Barbe butcher's shop without seeming to hear a whisper coming from somewhere very far away, urging you to go in. Grandpa was a real character – even though he's passed on, he's still somewhere in the shop.

And now my walking boots and I have been out and about on the high plateaux of the Ardèche – more accurately, in Saint-Agrève – for 38 years. Mum, you were really smart when you decided to be born there among the spruce trees on a bend in the winding road, far from the madding crowd. And a message to my readers: why not visit Saint-Agrève? It's well worth it, for although you have to negotiate sharp bends in the road, you get to breathe clean air at a height of 1,000 metres (3,300 feet). Spend some leisurely time here and you'll soon be a Saint-Agrève addict.

And finally, a note about my recipes. People cook differently in different parts of the world due to varying local ingredients and cooking customs. So that you can use the recipes in this book wherever you live, although I have sometimes listed French or other European ingredients (see the back of the book for descriptions of cheeses and wines), I have also included alternative ingredients whenever possible. Even so, some things may be more difficult to find in your local shops than others. In these cases don't be afraid to use a more readily available ingredient instead. If in doubt ask your butcher or greengrocer for help; they are usually a great source of information and should be able to point you in the right direction. As a result, the flavour of your dish may be slightly different from mine, but that's the beauty of cooking – it's alchemy at it's best!

BOUCHERIE - CHARCUTERIE

Spécialité Ardéchoise de Saucissons et Jambonnettes

R. BARBE

5, place de la République, 5
SAINT - AGRÈVE (Ardèche)

Stéphane

I was very small when Grandpa Barbe sat me on the cold imitation leather of the seat in his van and took me to visit the local farms. I had some unforgettable experiences there and became familiar with the festive atmosphere when a pig was slaughtered. It is 30 years since I first attended the ceremony and I can say that the tradition has endured. Nothing has really changed, apart from a few details as set out below.

7 YEARS OLD

FIRST SLAUGHTER

-12 °C (10 °F) outdoor temperature

1 hot chocolate

1 pig, weighing 180 kg (400 lb)

2 bales of straw

2 metres (6.5 feet) of black pudding

2 slices of bread and butter,
1 hot chocolate

60 cooking sausages

50 cured sausages

1 fricassée, 2 glasses
of Arcens mineral water

50 caillettes (Ardèche sausages)

20 kg (44 lb) pâté

8 kg (18 lb) roasting pork

2 hams

2 rolled breasts

40 YEARS OLD

LATEST SLAUGHTER

-12 °C (10 °F) outdoor temperature

2 glasses of white wine

1 pig, weighing 180 kg (400 lb)

2 bales of straw

2 metres (6.5 feet) of black pudding

Cheese, pâté,
3 glasses of white wine

60 cooking sausages

50 cured sausages

1 fricassée, 3 glasses
of red wine

50 caillettes (Ardèche sausages)

20 kg (44 lb) pâté

8 kg (18 lb) roasting pork

2 hams

2 rolled breasts

Before you read on . . .

February,

Saint-Agrève (on the high plateaux of the Ardèche),

-15 °C (5 °F), 7.00 a.m.

Pig-killing time at Saint-Agrève

Pig-Killing time at Saint-Agrève

IN PRAISE OF THE PIG

The ritual when a pig is slaughtered still has many good years ahead of it. It is fortunate that the standardization of flavour in today's food industry has not yet reached the high plateaux of the Ardèche region, where tradition mounts a good defence. Slaughtering and butchering call for precise organization. The team forms around the slaughterer – truly, the conductor of the orchestra. He makes incisions, cuts, saws; his assistants bone the meat, cut it up, chop it. The rhythm keeps going, interrupted only for good white wine and a few sausages that would make even the most ardent vegetarian's mouth water. Everyone lends a hand and shares in the spoils. It's a great experience!

Eric

ERIC'S PIGS ARE HAPPY PIGS

A pig is very small, about three weeks old, when it goes to stay at Eric's gourmet establishment to indulge in its favourite pastime – eating. It doesn't know it will be eaten itself in its own turn. Every meal is a porcine banquet, a three-star fattening-up programme, with a menu of whey, potatoes and cabbages. But this happy state of affairs doesn't last for ever, as the aim of the temporary pampering is to produce meat of the best quality, something that Eric does exceptionally well. No stress, plenty of space, lots and lots to eat – the pigs who pig out at his place are sure to tantalize any connoisseur's taste buds.

Pig-killing time at Saint-Agrève

AIMÉ LOVINGLY PRACTISES HIS TRADE

Used to making a whole battery of machine tools purr along, Aimé deals with an animal before you can say 'knife'. Moreover, he has been known for being sharp as a proverbial knife for several decades on many of the farms on the high plateaux. The pig family all acknowledge his expertise. Prince of the art of cutting up the carcass, lord of the black pudding, with his surgical skill he can transform a beast weighing 180 kg (400 lb) into a charcutier's display window within a morning. Nothing is left to chance when he has to deal with a mountain of meat, and sausages both large and small won't wait. Then Aimé turns into something like a Swiss watchmaker: working precisely, meticulously and fast (that's the only real difference between him and the Swiss watchmaker), he cuts up the carcass, frees the caul and intestines, ties joints, bones the meat, removes fat, carves and chops...all in time to an appreciative clicking of his tongue as he takes a glass of wine to help him in his labours.

For all the family . . .
when it's a big one!

3 kg (6½ lb) fresh pork fat
3 kg (6½ lb) onions, finely chopped
1 litre (1¾ pints) crème fraîche
300 ml (½ pint) cognac, marc or brandy
6 pinches of ground mixed spice
2 pinches of sugar
120 g (4 oz) salt
6 litres (10½ pints) pig's blood
a few metres of sausage casings
100 g (3½ oz) lard

Making
black pudding

Pig-killing time at Saint-Agrève

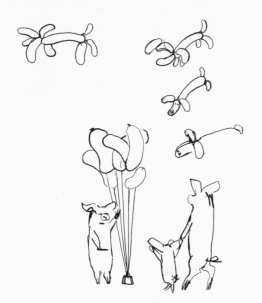

Heat 1 kg (2¼ lb) of the fat in a large pan. Add the onions and cook over a low heat, stirring occasionally, for about 20 minutes, until very soft.

Dice the remaining fat, mix with the softened onions and allow to partially melt. Add the crème fraîche, cognac, marc or brandy, spice, sugar and salt. Pour in the blood, stirring constantly to prevent it from congealing.

Using a funnel, gently fill the sausage casings. Cook the sausages in a large pan of gently simmering water (80°C/176°F) for 10 minutes.

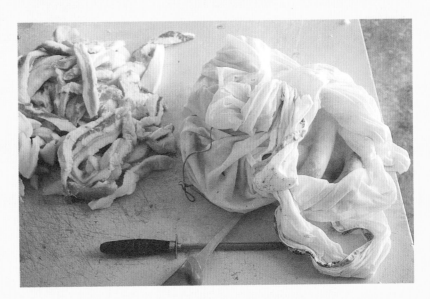

Remove the black puddings and grease them using a cloth spread with the lard.

This is a classic black pudding recipe which you can flavour however you like. Vary the ingredients freely by adding chopped chestnuts, apples, ground allspice or aniseed...

Remember to check that there are no holes in the sausage casings by inflating them (just as you'd blow up a balloon) before ladling in the mixture.

Blachou and Florette

AN INSEPARABLE COUPLE,
ALWAYS AROUND AT A PIG-KILLING

They appear at dawn as if by magic: Blachou with his woolly cap on and a smoking hand-rolled cigarette between his lips; Florette the dog, stomach nicely rounded by years of pig-killings, nose at ground level, taking in the festive atmosphere. They are always ready and willing to join the team, the centre of which – the pig – is still dreaming and unaware of its fate, its mind filled with large quantities of potatoes. For a pig dreams of nothing else, and fattens up even while it's asleep. This sweet vision is fleeting, however, and there's no time for sentimentality when Blachou goes into action. He calmly bones and cuts up the carcass, while Florette growls and snaps up anything that's going.

Pig-killing time at Saint-Agrève

BREAKING FOR A SNACK AT TEN O'CLOCK

A man without a knife will end up no more than mere skin and bone! Don't forget to bring a knife when you're working with a pig-killing team, so that you can help yourself to a chunk of crusty bread, a slice of sausage or a piece of Picodon goat's cheese.

Pierre and Charlou

BROTHERS WITH DEEP ROOTS
IN SAINT-JEAN-ROURE

These two brothers are the living history of peasant life. Welcome guests
at the pig-killing – they look after us and make sure we don't go thirsty –
Pierre and Charlou are like two oak trees that have been around for ever.
No one can imagine one without the other.

Time has no hold on their peaceful existence – they are no longer just part
of the landscape, they are the landscape.

Pig-killing time at Saint-Agrève

PERUSING THE NEWS AT A PIG-KILLING

A pig-killing gives you the chance to look through the *Dauphiné Libéré* newspaper. Like the pig itself, the paper is taken apart and devoured: every story is enriched with pithy comments. Immerse yourself in the *Dauphiné Libéré* and you'll soon feel you belong on the high plateaux of the Ardèche.

FRICASSÉE, HEARTY STEW FOR LUNCH

This is the time of day when the women, having collected their kids from school, join the men for lunch. Never mind a slimming diet of healthy carrots and steamed fish, they'll enjoy some real cooking for a change. The fricassée is delicious and brings colour to everyone's cheeks. It will sustain you through an afternoon of work, and the memory will live on until evening.

A short lesson in anatomy

leg

trotter

loin

shoulder   blade

Pig-killing time at Saint-Agrève

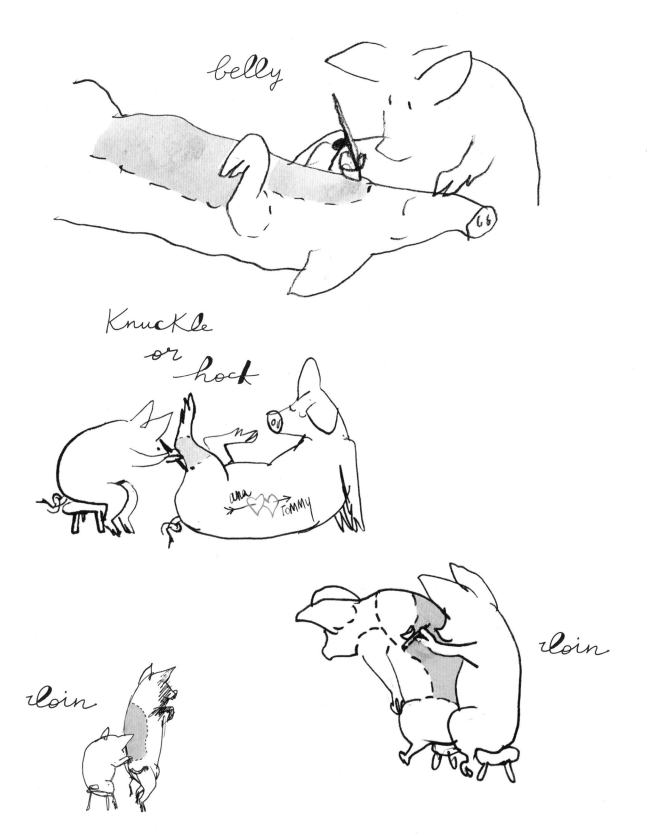

Black pudding recipes

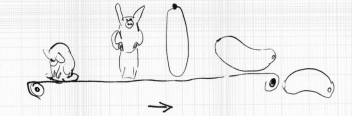

fricassée

PREPARATION TIME: 20 MINUTES
COOKING TIME: 30 MINUTES

SERVES 6

100 g (3½ oz) lard or unsalted butter
2 large onions, thinly sliced
6 Charlotte or other waxy potatoes, thinly sliced into rounds
200 g (7 oz) pig's liver, cut into cubes
2 pig's kidneys, cut into cubes
200 g (7 oz) pig's heart, cut into cubes
800 g (1¾ lb) black pudding, cut into cubes
1 bunch of fresh parsley, chopped
3 garlic cloves, chopped
salt and pepper

Melt the lard or butter in a large pan over a low heat. Add the onions and potatoes and cook, stirring gently, for 10–15 minutes, until lightly browned. Stir in the liver, kidneys and heart and cook until evenly browned. Add the black pudding and cook until it has heated through, then remove the pan from the heat.

Sprinkle the parsley and garlic over the fricassée, season to taste with salt and pepper and serve immediately, straight from the pan.

black pudding with walnuts and chestnuts

PREPARATION TIME: 5 MINUTES
COOKING TIME: 30 MINUTES

SERVES 6

8 shallots
8 garlic cloves
175 ml (6 fl oz) milk
3 tablespoons olive oil
175 ml (6 fl oz) dry white wine
2 teaspoons canned veal or beef stock
400 g (14 oz) peeled chestnuts, thawed if frozen
100 g (3½ oz) shelled walnuts
300 ml (½ pint) double cream
800 g (1¾ lb) black pudding
salt and pepper

Peel the shallots and garlic but leave them whole. Put the garlic in a pan, add the milk and simmer gently. Heat the olive oil in another pan, add the shallots and cook, stirring occasionally, for 10–15 minutes, until evenly browned.

Meanwhile, heat the wine in a third pan. Mix the veal or beef stock with the wine, add to the shallots and cook until reduced. Drain the garlic and add it to the pan along with the chestnuts and walnuts, then pour in the cream, heat through and season to taste with salt and pepper. The sauce should have a syrupy consistency.

Remove the skin from the black pudding, cut it in half lengthways and cook it in a frying pan.

Serve the two black pudding halves topped with the shallot and nut garnish.

black pudding
with autumn fruits

PREPARATION TIME: 15 MINUTES
COOKING TIME: 30 MINUTES

SERVES 6

6 firm pears
2 pinches of ground cinnamon
3 quinces
100 g (3½ oz) lard or unsalted butter
6 Cox's Orange Pippins or other small eating apples
800 g (1¾ lb) black pudding
2 tablespoons sugar
100 g (3½ oz) peeled chestnuts in vacuum pack or jar
2 tablespoons Calvados
salt and pepper

Peel the pears and coat with the cinnamon. Core the quinces and cut into quarters.

Melt half the lard or butter over a very low heat. Add the quinces and cook for 10 minutes, turning occasionally until lightly browned.

Meanwhile, core and halve the apples. Add to the pan along with the pears, and turn to coat.

Melt the remaining lard or butter in a frying pan. Remove the skin from the black pudding, add the pudding to the frying pan and heat through. Keep warm.

When the fruit starts to soften, add the sugar and chestnuts and cook until caramelized. Add the Calvados and heat for 1 minute, then ignite. When the flames have died down, season to taste with salt and pepper.

Serve the black pudding accompanied by the three fruits and the flambéed cooking liquid.

black pudding gratin
with caramelized onions

PREPARATION TIME: 40 MINUTES
COOKING TIME: 30 MINUTES

SERVES 6

800 g (1¾ lb) floury potatoes
150 g (5 oz) slightly salted butter
1 teaspoon freshly grated nutmeg
4 tablespoons olive oil
6 onions, sliced
100 g (3½ oz) lardons
100 g (3½ oz) shelled hazelnuts
1 bunch of fresh tarragon, chopped
800 g (1¾ lb) black pudding
2 slices of toast, crumbled
salt and pepper

Cook the potatoes in a large pan of lightly salted boiling water for 15–20 minutes, until tender. Drain well, mash with a fork and beat in the butter and nutmeg. Season to taste with salt and pepper.

Meanwhile, heat the olive oil in a large pan. Add the onions and cook over a low heat, stirring occasionally, for 20 minutes, until very soft. Stir in the lardons and hazelnuts and cook, stirring frequently, until browned. Add the tarragon.

Preheat the oven to 180°C (350°F/Gas Mark 4).

Remove the skin from the black pudding and cut it into 1 cm (5 inch) slices. Cook in a frying pan, turning occasionally, until caramelized.

Place half the mashed potatoes in a gratin dish and cover with all the onions. Place the black pudding slices on top and cover with the remaining mashed potatoes.

Sprinkle with the toast crumbs and bake in the oven until the topping is golden brown.

black pudding, apple, potato and fennel tart

PREPARATION TIME: 50 MINUTES
COOKING TIME: 20 MINUTES

SERVES 6

3 shallots, thinly sliced
4 tablespoons crème fraîche
3 tablespoons olive oil, plus extra for drizzling
4 Charlotte or other waxy potatoes
2 eating apples
100 g (3½ oz) smoked lardons, rindless
400 g (14 oz) black pudding
350 g (12 oz) puff pastry dough, thawed if frozen
plain flour, for dusting
¼ fennel bulb, thinly sliced
1 bunch of rocket, optional, torn into pieces
salt and pepper

Mix together the shallots and crème fraîche in a bowl. Add 1 tablespoon of the olive oil and season with salt and pepper. Set aside.

Cook the potatoes in lightly salted boiling water for 15–20 minutes, until tender. Drain well, then cut into thin rounds. Preheat the grill.

Peel, core and slice the apples. Heat the remaining olive oil in a frying pan, add the apple slices and cook until they are just beginning to colour.

Spread out the lardons on a baking sheet and cook under the grill, turning once, for 5–8 minutes, until tender. Meanwhile, remove the skin from the black pudding and cut into thin slices.

Preheat the oven to 180°C (350°F/Gas Mark 4).

Roll out the puff pastry dough on a lightly floured surface to a 25 cm (10 inch) round and place on a baking sheet. Spread 2 tablespoons of the shallot cream evenly over the dough round. Sprinkle with the fennel and lardons, then arrange alternate layers of black pudding, potato and apple slices on top. Cover with the remaining shallot cream. Bake in the oven for 20 minutes.

Cover the tart with the rocket, if using, drizzle with olive oil and serve immediately.

black pudding crostini with pears and beetroot

PREPARATION TIME: 30 MINUTES
TO ASSEMBLE: 10 MINUTES

MAKES 12

6 tablespoons olive oil
2 garlic cloves, coarsely chopped
3 pears
10 g (¼ oz) unsalted butter
12 slices of pain de campagne or rustic bread
200 g (7 oz) black pudding, cut into 5 mm (¼ inch) slices
1 cooked beetroot, cut into thin batons
fresh chives, to garnish

Heat the olive oil in a frying pan. Add the garlic and cook until it is just beginning to colour. Remove the garlic with a slotted spoon and discard. Set aside the pan of flavoured olive oil.

Peel and core the pears, then cut each into eighths. Melt the butter in another frying pan, add the pears and cook over a low heat, turning occasionally, until golden brown.

Heat the garlic-flavoured olive oil, add the bread slices, in batches, and cook until golden brown on both sides. Drain on kitchen paper.

Meanwhile, cook the slices of black pudding in another pan until lightly browned on both sides.

Divide the pieces of pear, the beetroot batons and black pudding slices among the slices of fried bread and garnish with the chives.

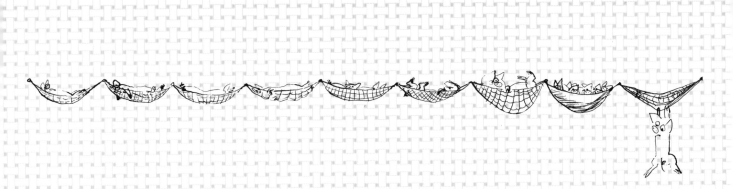

For the love of sausages

SAUSAGES

WHAT ARE THEY?

A fresh sausage is a meat-filled casing. The casing is traditionally made from an intestine and it is filled with a mixture of finely or coarsely chopped meat, including both fat and lean meat, and seasoned to taste. Seasoning is particularly important in making sausages. The word sausage – and its French equivalents *saucisse* and *saucisson* – is ultimately derived from the Latin *salsus*, meaning 'salted'.

DO YOU SPEAK SAUSAGE?

Many regions throughout France have their own sausage recipes and the sausages, in turn, take their names from these regions. From Savoy to Toulouse sausages and from Strasbourg *knack* to Montbéliard *saucisse*, sausage is named in the same way as cheese. Its identity is locked into its region, giving it a distinctive shape and character: spiced or smoked, coarse or fine, plain or herb-flavoured, mixed with other meats or consisting solely of pork, it is a tribute to the pork butcher's skill.

Of course, sausages are not only an icon of French gastronomy, as most other countries have their own culinary traditions too.

Germany alone has over 1,500 varieties of *Wurst*, including the famous Frankfurter, known to all fans of hot dogs and a real transatlantic star.

The great British breakfast would not be complete without the aroma of grilled sausages and the famous Spanish *chorizo* sets international taste buds tingling with its peppery seasoning. Italy and Hungary produce fabulous salami too …

It would take an encyclopaedia in several volumes to cover all the different kinds of sausages and their local names in detail.

Making
small sausages

Making large
slicing sausages

63

THREE TYPES OF SAUSAGES

SAUSAGES FOR GRILLING

Godiveaux	Small casing, 20 cm (8 inches) long, fine texture
Chipolata	Small casing, 20 cm (8 inches) long, fine texture, often flavoured with herbs
Paysanne	Medium casing, 15 cm (6 inches) long, coarse texture
Toulouse	Medium casing, 15 cm (6 inches) long, fine texture

SAUSAGES FOR POACHING

Paysanne	Medium casing, 15 cm (6 inches) long, coarse texture
Frankfurter	Small casing, 15 cm (6 inches) long, smooth texture, can be smoked
Strasbourg	Small casing, 15 cm (6 inches) long, smooth texture, may contain beef, often coloured red
Saveloy	Large casing, 25 cm (10 inches) long, fine texture, may contain truffles and pistachios and is served in slices
Montbéliard	Small casing, 15 cm (6 inches) long, fine texture, flavoured with cumin and shallots, smoked
Morteau	Large casing, 25 cm (10 inches) long, coarse texture, smoked, secured with twine

SAUSAGES FOR SPREADING

Strichtwurscht	Large casing, 15 cm (6 inches) long, fine texture, often with pig's liver (Lewerwurscht), flavoured with cumin and paprika, smoked
Soubressade	Large beef casing, fine stuffing with large pieces, often flavoured with pepper

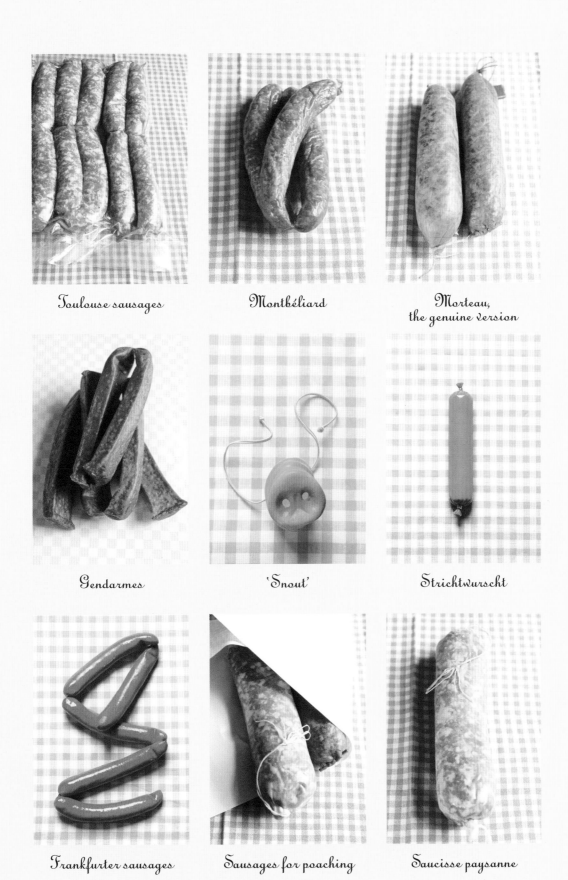

Toulouse sausages

Montbéliard

Morteau,
the genuine version

Gendarmes

'Snout'

Strichtwurscht

Frankfurter sausages

Sausages for poaching

Saucisse paysanne

CURED SAUSAGES

'How do you get to be a cured sausage?,' asked one of the usual cooking variety, not yet wrinkled by maturing.

Large cured sausages for slicing, the equivalent of Italian salami, are very popular because they are so easy to keep and serve. As they are rich in proteins and lipids, they are ideal for snacks.

MAKING CURED SAUSAGES

Cured sausages are made in the same way as cooking sausages. The natural intestines of the pig are used as casings and filled with a mixture of fat and lean pork. Then they are cured. Unlike cooking sausages, the slicing sausage develops its character through malo-lactic fermentation, which is sometimes encouraged by drying at 25°C (77°F) for 24 hours. The process of transformation then begins. Once removed from the drying room, the sausage naturally develops micro-organisms which help its flavours to become concentrated.

MATURING AND DRYING

The maturing and drying stage is very important. The rate at which water evaporates from the sausage has to be checked regularly to prevent a crust from forming. This happens when evaporation is too fast and is a problem because the crust will prevent the remaining water from evaporating. On the other hand, evaporation that is too slow creates a sticky formation on the surface, which also prevents the rest of the water from evaporating.

Cured sausages develop and mature rather like a good wine. Depending on the shape and size of the sausage, drying lasts from five to eight weeks, but the length of the process is largely determined by the consumer's taste. The sausage-maker's finances also play a role as the shorter the maturing period, the heavier the sausage will be. Cured sausages, once matured, will have lost 20 per cent of their original weight.

ANDOUILLE, ANDOUILLETTE, VIRE

The huge sausage family contains other kinds too, including andouille and andouillette. These are cooked sausages basically consisting of pig chitterlings, usually smoked and then dried. The best known come from Vire in Normandy and Guémené in Brittany. The basis of andouillettes is pig's tripe and intestines, cooked and then filled into a casing. And then there are Danish and Hungarian salami, Italian mortadella…

Jésus — a large pork sausage from Franche-Comté

THE CURED SAUSAGE FAMILY

Rosette Casing known as 'rosette' with a spindle shape, 40–50 cm (16–20 inches) long, 800 g–1.2 kg (1¾–2½ lb), medium texture, dried for 8 weeks

Jésus Casing known as *sac de porc*, 30 cm (12 inches) long, thick, 900 g–1.3 kg (2–3 lb), medium texture, dried for 8–10 weeks

Saucisson Chaudin, 20–25 cm (8–10 inches) long, texture often coarse, 300–500 g (11 oz–1 lb 2 oz), dried for 6 weeks

Saucisse sèche Also know as Lorraine, long casing, 50 cm (20 inches), medium texture, U shape, dried for 2–3 weeks

Salami Chaudin, fine and relatively fat texture, 800 g–1.5 kg (1¾–3¼ lb), can be cooked or dried

Mortadella Large synthetic casing, smooth texture, cooked with pieces of fat, can be matured with wine, flavoured with pistachios and coriander seeds, 1–100 kg (2¼–225 lb)

Chorizo Long or large casing, U shape or large sausage, medium texture, enhanced with paprika and garlic

For the love of sausages

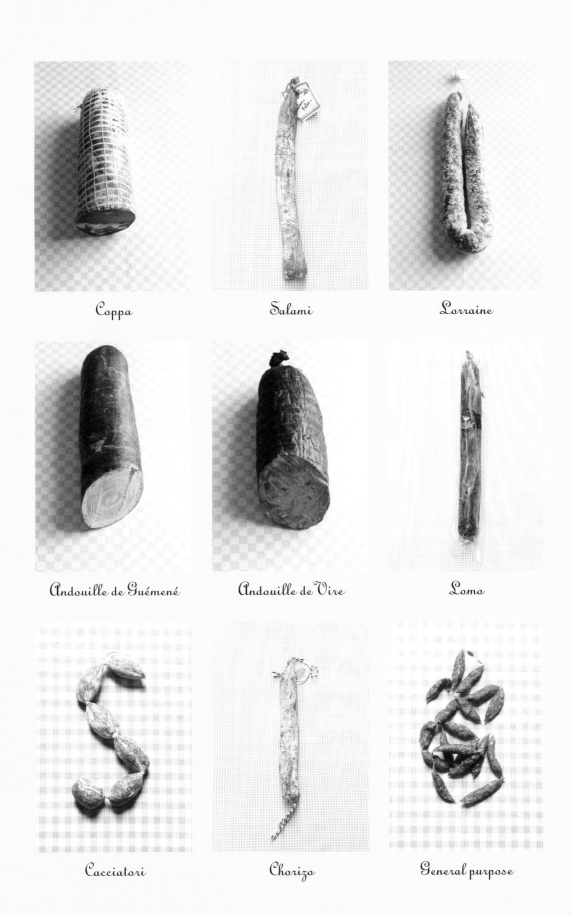

Coppa

Salami

Lorraine

Andouille de Guémené

Andouille de Vire

Lomo

Cacciatori

Chorizo

General purpose

Sausage recipes

Sausage cassoulet

SOAKING TIME: 24 HOURS
PREPARATION TIME: 15 MINUTES
COOKING TIME: 4 HOURS

SERVES 6

400 g (14 oz) dried haricot beans, soaked in cold water for 24 hours and drained
1 onion
1 carrot
3 garlic cloves
2 bay leaves
1 tablespoon veal or beef stock powder (whenever 1 tablespoon
   of stock powder is used in this book, you could use 2 stock cubes instead)
6 ripe tomatoes, quartered
100 g (3½ oz) fresh pork rind, sliced, or lardons
1 litre (1¾ pints) dry white wine
6 saucisses paysannes (see pages 64 and 65) or country-style sausages
2 slices of toast, crumbled
100 g (3½ oz) duck fat, melted

Bring a pan of water to simmering point and add the beans, onion, carrot, garlic and bay leaves. Simmer for 2 hours, then drain and reserve the cooking liquid. Discard the flavourings. Stir in the stock powder and add the tomatoes. Preheat the oven to 160°C (325°F/Gas Mark 3).

Place the beans in a terracotta dish and add the pork rind or lardons. Pour in the white wine and enough of the reserved cooking liquid and tomatoes almost to fill the dish. Prick the sausages and push them down into the mixture. Bake in the oven for 2 hours, adding more of the cooking liquid and tomatoes if necessary to prevent the mixture from drying out.

Preheat the grill. Sprinkle the cassoulet with the toast crumbs, pour the melted duck fat over them and grill briefly before serving.

CASSOULET

Cassoulet is a rich, slow-cooked bean stew containing meat (usually pork sausages, pork, goose and duck), and haricot beans.

For the love of sausages

Sausage confit with split peas

PREPARATION TIME: 10 MINUTES
COOKING TIME: 2½ HOURS

SERVES 6

500 g (1 lb 2 oz) split peas
1 onion
1 leek
1 bunch of fresh coriander
3 fresh thyme sprigs
1 large rind sausage (to be ordered from your butcher) or other large sausage
1 tablespoon veal or beef stock powder
200 ml (7 fl oz) double cream

Bring a large pan of water to simmering point. Add the split peas, onion, leek, coriander and thyme and cook for 1 hour. Add the sausage and stock powder and simmer for 1 hour more.

Drain the peas but leave the sausage in the cooking liquid. Place the peas in a flameproof casserole, strain in enough of the cooking liquid to cover, add the sausage and pour in the cream. Cook over a very low heat for about 30 minutes.

Split open the sausage lengthways and serve straight from the casserole. The sausagemeat should be served with a spoon.

For the love of sausages

Montbéliard sausage gratin and vegetable tian with thyme

PREPARATION TIME: 20 MINUTES
COOKING TIME: 1 HOUR

SERVES 6

2 aubergines, cut into thin rounds
6 tomatoes, cut into thin rounds
4 courgettes, cut into thin rounds
3 large onions, cut into thin rounds
6 fresh thyme sprigs, leaves only
4 bay leaves
6 garlic cloves, coarsely chopped
175 ml (6 fl oz) white wine
100 ml (3½ fl oz) olive oil
20 g (¾ oz) unsalted butter
6 Montbéliard sausages (see pages 64 and 65) or
  other small smoked sausages
sea salt

Preheat the oven to 160°C (325°F/Gas Mark 3).

Place all the vegetable rounds vertically, in layers, in a casserole. Add the thyme leaves, bay leaves, garlic, white wine, olive oil and butter. Prick the sausages and arrange them on the top.

Cover and bake in the oven for 1 hour, until the vegetables are very tender. Season with sea salt and serve.

For the love of sausages

Warm sausage and Puy lentil salad with herb marinade

PREPARATION TIME: 25 MINUTES
COOKING TIME: 40 MINUTES

SERVES 6

500 g (1 lb 2 oz) Puy lentils
1 bouquet garni
2 large sausages
50 g (2 oz) smoked lardons, cut into thin batons
1 teaspoon Dijon mustard
a dash of balsamic vinegar
100 ml (3½ fl oz) walnut oil
1 shallot, preferably grey, chopped
3 fresh tarragon sprigs

FOR THE MARINADE

100 ml (3½ fl oz) walnut oil
6 fresh chives, finely chopped
2 fresh tarragon sprigs, finely chopped
1 shallot, preferably grey, finely chopped
1 tablespoon chopped hazelnuts

Mix together all the marinade ingredients in a bowl and set aside until required.

Place the lentils, bouquet garni and sausages in a pan and add plenty of water. Simmer over a low heat for 40 minutes.

Meanwhile, preheat the grill. Spread out the lardons on a baking sheet and grill, turning once, until golden.

Make a vinaigrette by mixing together the mustard, balsamic vinegar, walnut oil and grilled lardons.

Remove the sausages from the pan and slice. Discard the bouquet garni. Drain and rinse the lentils, place in a bowl and add the vinaigrette, shallot and tarragon.

Place a dome of lentils in the centre of each individual serving plate, surround with slices of warm sausage and coat with the marinade. Serve immediately.

Sausage in brioche

PREPARATION TIME: 20 MINUTES PLUS 30 MINUTES FOR RISING
COOKING TIME: 40 MINUTES

SERVES 6

4 eggs
300 g (11 oz) plain flour
2 teaspoons baking powder
200 ml (7 fl oz) double cream
100 ml (3½ fl oz) milk
50 g (2 oz) shelled pistachio nuts
50 g (2 oz) grilled lardons
1 cooked sausage or saveloy (see page 64)

Beat the eggs in a bowl until thoroughly combined. Sift the flour with the baking powder into another bowl, then gradually beat in the eggs and pour in the cream and milk to make a smooth dough. Mix the pistachios and lardons into the dough.

Half-fill a non-stick loaf tin with the dough, place the sausage along the centre and cover with the remaining dough. Leave to rise in a warm place for 30 minutes.

Meanwhile, preheat the oven to 200°C (400°F/Gas Mark 6).

Bake the loaf in the oven for 40 minutes. Turn out on to a wire rack to cool.

Serve in slices with a well-seasoned frisée salad.

For the love of sausages

Sabodet with Mâcon wine, vegetables and dried mushrooms

PREPARATION TIME: 40 MINUTES
COOKING TIME: 40 MINUTES

SERVES 6

50 g (2 oz) dried porcini mushrooms
4 fresh parsley sprigs
3 garlic cloves
2 shallots, chopped
6 carrots, cut into cubes
6 baby turnips, cut into quarters
½ celeriac, cut into cubes
200 g (7 oz) chestnut mushrooms
1 sabodet sausage, large rind sausage (to be ordered
  from your butcher) or other large sausage
500 ml (18 fl oz) white Mâcon wine or other young French Burgundy (Chardonnay)

Place the dried mushrooms in a bowl, add warm water to cover and leave to soak for 25–30 minutes. Meanwhile, remove the leaves from the parsley sprigs and reserve the stalks. Chop 1 of the garlic cloves with the parsley leaves. Drain the porcinis and cook them in a frying pan with the parsley and garlic mixture.

Place the shallots, carrots, turnips, celeriac, chestnut mushrooms, porcini mushroom mixture, parsley stalks and remaining garlic cloves in a flameproof casserole. Add the sausage and pour in the white wine. Cover and cook over a low heat for 40 minutes.

Skim off any fat from the surface with a ladle and then serve straight from the casserole.

SABODET AND MÂCON

A speciality of Lyon, sabodet sausages are pork sausages made from pig's head and skin. They have a strong, earthy flavour. Mâcon wines are red and white wines from the Mâconnais part of Burgundy, France.

For the love of sausages

Warm Morteau sausage with Roseval potato, carrot and celery salad

PREPARATION TIME: 30 MINUTES
COOKING TIME: 40 MINUTES

SERVES 6

2 Morteau sausages (see pages 64 and 65)
  or other large smoked sausages
1 carrot
1 celery stick, cut into thin batons
1 shallot, finely chopped
100 ml (3½ fl oz) olive oil
1 tablespoon balsamic vinegar
6 Roseval or other red-skinned,
  yellow-fleshed potatoes, unpeeled
coarsely ground black pepper

Place the Morteau sausages in a saucepan of water and bring to the boil, then lower the heat and simmer for 20 minutes.

Meanwhile, halve the carrot lengthways and cut into thin strips using a vegetable peeler. Put the carrot strips, celery and shallot in a bowl. Whisk together the olive oil and balsamic vinegar in a jug and season to taste with pepper. Pour two-thirds of the dressing over the vegetables and toss lightly, then set aside.

Add the potatoes to the saucepan, bring back to the boil and simmer gently for a further 20 minutes, until the potatoes are tender and the sausages are cooked through. Remove the sausages and drain the potatoes, then slice both into rounds. Divide the potatoes and sausages among individual serving plates, drizzle the remaining dressing over the potatoes and top with the vegetable mixture.

Morteau sausage and smoked bacon with fresh salsify and shallot

PREPARATION TIME: 20 MINUTES
COOKING TIME: 40 MINUTES

SERVES 6

2 Morteau sausages (see pages 64 and 65) or
   other large smoked sausages
6 pear shallots or other elongated shallots
olive oil, for drizzling
juice of 1 lemon
1 kg (2¼ lb) salsify
50 g (2 oz) slightly salted butter
1 tablespoon sugar
1 tablespoon veal or beef stock powder,
   mixed with 500 ml (18 fl oz) boiling water
6 rashers of smoked bacon

Poach the sausages in gently simmering water for 40 minutes.

Meanwhile, preheat the oven to 180°C (350°F/Gas Mark 4).

Place the shallots in an ovenproof dish, drizzle with olive oil and bake for 20 minutes, until they feel springy to the touch.

Stir the lemon juice into a bowl of water. Working on one root at a time, peel the salsify, cut it into even short lengths and immediately place it in the acidulated water to prevent discoloration. Drain the salsify, place in a sauté pan, add the butter, sugar and veal or beef stock mixture and pour in enough water to cover.

Meanwhile, preheat the grill.

Cook the salsify over a low heat until it is glazed and shiny golden brown. Grill the bacon for 2–4 minutes on each side, until lightly browned.

Drain the sausages and slice. Make a bed of salsify on six individual serving plates. Cover with the sliced sausages, the bacon and, finally, the shallots split open lengthways. Spoon over the salsify cooking juices and serve.

For the love of sausages

Andouille and dandelion salad

PREPARATION TIME: 10 MINUTES

SERVES 6

100 ml (3½ fl oz) olive oil
2 garlic cloves, chopped
1 tablespoon cider vinegar
1 teaspoon clear honey
300 g (11 oz) dandelion leaves
24 slices of Vire andouille sausage
  (see pages 66 and 69)

Heat the olive oil in a small frying pan. Add the garlic and cook briefly, then remove the pan from the heat. Stir in the vinegar and honey.

Wash the dandelion leaves and spin or pat dry. Place in a bowl and toss with the warm vinaigrette.

Make a small bed of dandelion leaves on each of six serving plates and top with a slice of sausage. Continue making layers in this way until all the ingredients are used up, then serve.

If the unique andouille sausages are unavailable, another sausage of similar size can be used, but the flavour will differ slightly.

For the love of sausages

Grilled Guémené andouille sausage with vegetable mirepoix

PREPARATION TIME: 30 MINUTES
COOKING TIME: 20 MINUTES

SERVES 6

120 ml (4 fl oz) olive oil
2 garlic cloves, chopped
5 cm (2 inch) piece of fresh root ginger, chopped
4 very ripe tomatoes, cut into quarters
1 teaspoon tomato ketchup
3 shallots, chopped
1 celeriac, diced
2 aubergines, diced
2 courgettes, diced
2 onions, sliced
18 thick slices of Guémené andouille sausage (see pages 66 and 69)

Heat 2 tablespoons of the olive oil in a pan. Add the garlic and ginger and cook, stirring frequently, for a few minutes. Add the tomatoes and cook over a low heat, stirring occasionally, for about 20 minutes, until pulpy. Stir in the ketchup, transfer the mixture to a food processor and process to a thick and smooth coulis. Preheat the grill.

Heat 4 tablespoons of the remaining oil in a large pan. Add the shallots and celeriac and cook, stirring occasionally, for about 10 minutes, then add the aubergines and cook for a few minutes more, then add the courgettes. Cook until the vegetables are tender crisp. Meanwhile, heat the remaining oil in another pan and cook the sliced onions for 5–10 minutes. Grill the slices of sausage.

To serve, form a dome of the vegetables on individual serving plates, top with alternating slices of sausage and fried onions and garnish with the tomato coulis.

If andouille sausages are unavailable, use a sausage of similar size.

MIREPOIX

This is a classic preparation of basic ingredients (onions, carrots, celery, and sometimes herbs). Mirepoix can be eaten raw, but is often sautéed in butter and used as the flavour base for sauces, soups and stews or as a bed on which to cook meat or fish.

For the love of sausages

Herb-marinated sausage

PREPARATION TIME: 5 MINUTES
MARINATING TIME: 1 WEEK

SERVES 1 AS AN APPETIZER

1 mature cured sausage, such as chorizo
1 garlic clove
10 juniper berries
2 fresh thyme sprigs
1 bay leaf
a pinch of fresh rosemary
300–600 ml (½–1 pint) olive oil
toasted bread, to serve

Slice the sausage and remove the skin. Place the sausage slices in a preserving jar with the garlic, juniper berries, thyme, bay leaf and rosemary. Add olive oil to cover, close the lid and leave in the refrigerator for at least 1 week.

Serve the sausage with a slice of toasted bread.

chorizo and mozzarella tapas

PREPARATION TIME: 10 MINUTES
COOKING TIME: 5 MINUTES

MAKES 10

2 slices of toast, crumbled
100 g (3½ oz) ground almonds
2 eggs
10 small mozzarella cheeses
10 fresh basil leaves
10 thin slices of spicy chorizo sausage
oil, for deep-frying

Mix together the toast crumbs and ground almonds in a shallow dish. Beat the eggs well in another shallow dish. Roll the mozzarella cheeses first in the egg and then in the toast and almond mixture. Repeat this process three times.

Place each mozzarella cheese on a wooden cocktail stick and add a basil leaf and a slice of chorizo.

Heat the oil in a large pan, add the tapas and fry for 15 seconds. Drain well and serve warm.

For the love of sausages

grilled chorizo and fresh herb salad

PREPARATION TIME: 15 MINUTES
COOKING TIME: 5 MINUTES

SERVES 6

1 bunch of fresh chervil
1 bunch of fresh tarragon
1 bunch of fresh coriander
1 bunch of fresh flat-leaf parsley
1 bunch of rocket
1 handful of wild dandelion or escarole leaves
12 slices of chorizo sausage, cut into thin batons
2 tablespoons wine vinegar
6 tablespoons rapeseed oil
2 red onions, sliced into thin rings

Coarsely tear the herb leaves from their stalks and mix them with the salad leaves in a bowl. Heat a griddle pan, add the chorizo and cook for a few minutes. Stir the wine vinegar into the cooking juices.

Add the oil to the salad and toss lightly. Add the chorizo and cooking juices and garnish with the onion rings.

Chorizo tortilla

PREPARATION TIME: 20 MINUTES
COOKING TIME: 20 MINUTES

SERVES 6

120 ml (4 fl oz) olive oil, plus extra for brushing
600 g (1 lb 5 oz) small potatoes, cut into large cubes
200 g (7 oz) chorizo sausage, cut into strips
3 onions, sliced
5 eggs
100 ml (3½ fl oz) double cream

Preheat the oven to 120°C (250°F/Gas Mark ½). Brush an ovenproof dish with oil.

Heat 5 tablespoons of the olive oil in a frying pan. Add the potatoes and cook over a medium heat for about 8 minutes, until just beginning to colour. Meanwhile, heat the remaining oil in another pan. Add the chorizo and onions and cook over a low heat, stirring occasionally, for 5 minutes, until the onions have softened. Mix together the onions, chorizo and potatoes. Beat the eggs until foaming, then add the cream.

Spoon the chorizo mixture into the prepared dish and pour over the beaten eggs to cover. Bake in the oven for 15–20 minutes, until golden brown and cooked through. Test by inserting the point of a sharp knife – it should come out dry. (You could also make several smaller tortillas, as pictured, but you will need to reduce the cooking time.)

Hamming it up

A little more ham, if you please!

COOKED HAM

A KIND OF HAM MISHMASH

'From the traditional French ham sandwich to the minced ham given to tiny children, every French citizen eats an average 5 kg (11 lb) cooked ham a year. Its nutritional benefits – rich in iron and potassium, low in fats for a pork product – and its versatility make it a permanent resident in all self-respecting refrigerators.

Cooked ham is made from the hind legs of the pig, which can be boned and moulded to shape, trimmed of fat and skinned, cured in brine and slow-cooked by a variety of techniques. French shops sell three kinds of cooked ham; 'superior' cooked ham is prepared without phosphates or gelling agents. Your butcher will also sell several varieties. Ask his advice if you need to find an alternative for any of the following recipes.

DISTINGUISHING BETWEEN FRENCH SUPERIOR HAMS

When ham cooked on the bone is called York ham or Prague ham, the name does not refer to the place where it was produced, but to its method of preparation and cooking.

Braised ham	Ham that has been slowly cooked.
Au torchon	Ham boned and cooked in broth (cooked in a cloth).
Ardennes ham	A pear-shaped ham.
Jambon de Paris	Can be recognized by its rectangular shape. (Not all jambon de Paris is of superior quality, so make sure you ask your butcher for the best he has.)
'Choice' ham	Boned and moulded ham made without gelling agents.
'Standard' ham	Boned and moulded ham made with some additives not permitted in the others.

'Snout'

DRY-CURED HAMS

The food of kings in the ancient world, dry-cured hams have made ham a real star, ennobling the art of charcuterie. Their high reputation is the outcome of very careful work in rearing pigs and producing ham. You don't get good hams without good pigs. The choice of breed and the way the animals are fattened are essential to producing high-quality hams. Uncooked ham is prepared by dry-salting the surface of the haunch. This salting, often done by hand, dries out the meat to improve its keeping quality. It is at this point that some producers add aromatic herbs and spices to give the ham character.

The hams are then put in special drying rooms where ventilation, temperature and humidity are carefully controlled so that the ham can mature in the best possible conditions.

Now the ham begins its process of transformation. The salt permeates the meat and matures it. It turns an intense red and develops its aroma as the process speeds up. The maturing and drying period varies according to the kind of ham; a good dry-cured variety can't be made from just any old ham.

Superior dry-cured ham: matured for a minimum of 210 days.

Dry-cured ham: matured for a minimum of 130 days.

Uncooked ham: matured for less than 130 days.

BAYONNE HAM

Bayonne ham can be produced only in the 22 *départements* of Aquitaine. The pigs, monitored from birth, are fed entirely on cereals and the haunches are rigorously selected before becoming hams. The climate of south-western France, between the ocean and the Pyrenees and subject to great variations in humidity, is the essential factor in maturing the ham and gives it a succulent texture. Other French hams have made a reputation outside their native country, including Auvergne ham, Savoy ham, Ardennes ham and Vendée ham.

Serrano

San Daniele

Speck

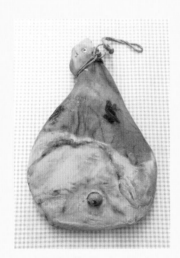

Parma

Bayonne ham

Dehesa de Extremadura

JAMÓN DE CERDO

Serrano ham, produced in Spain, has a worldwide reputation. The name simply refers to the word *sierra*, meaning 'mountain'. In fact, the special quality of Serrano ham is that its production follows the pattern of the mountain climate. The pigs are slaughtered and the meat is cured in winter, then it is dried during a period of changing temperatures as summer approaches, acquiring its characteristic flavour. The specifications for Serrano ham state that it is a traditional speciality subject to certain regulations, but do not guarantee the origin of the pigs or the place where the ham is produced. Spain produces one of the best hams in the world from *pata negra* ('black hoof') pigs. These wonderful hams bear the appellation Iberico, and the best Iberico ham is called *bellota*. The word *bellota*, meaning acorn, indicates that the pigs are free-range animals fattened among oak trees, where they feed entirely on acorns, doubling their weight during their time in the forest. The climate – cold winters, hot summers – and the process of maturing for a minimum of 24 months give both the fat and the lean meat of the ham an inimitable texture and aroma.

PROSCIUTTO DI MAIALE

Italy too can claim an ancient tradition in the making of its hams. The quality of Italian ham is recognized and appreciated by all gourmets. Prosciutto di Parma, a real gastronomic treat, results from extremely rigorous expertise and techniques. The breed of pig used is the Large White Landrace or Duroc, weighing at least 160 kg (350 lb), born and reared in 11 regions of Italy. The diet selected, the conditions in which it is reared, everything is done according to specifications that guarantee the high quality of the ham. The particular flavour of prosciutto di Parma comes from the art of the master curers, the heirs to several centuries of experience. They use very little salt, which means that the ham dries more slowly. After 12 months it will finally be revealed whether it is worthy to bear the sign of the ducal crown with its five points, the official guarantee that the meat conforms to specifications. This sign is awarded only after careful checking, a process called *spillatura*. The ham is checked in five specific places to confirm that it has matured successfully.

In northern Italy, prosciutto di San Daniele is made from large pigs weighing 200 kg (440 lb), reared exclusively in the Veneto, Piedmont and Lombardy. San Daniele hams are matured for ten months, so their meat is paler than that from Parma, and the trotter is left on the ham. Other hams such as the Bosses ham from the Val d'Aosta complete this rich tradition of charcuterie.

SCHINKEN AND SPECK

Germany, Austria and Belgium have their own skills in maturing hams too. Their methods may be lesser known, but the end products are certainly of high quality. Ardennes ham, Black Forest ham and Austrian Speck long ago became popular outside their own regions.

Dry-cured Auvergne ham:
mmm, very good.

LABELS DESIGNATING QUALITY

THREE DESIGNATIONS OF QUALITY IN EUROPE TO PROTECT AGRICULTURAL VARIETY AND DEFEND HAMS AGAINST IMITATIONS

PDO

Protected designation of origin guaranteed

Ham produced, developed and matured in a defined geographical area with recognized and confirmed expertise.

Spain
Dehesa de Extremadura Guijuelo

Jamón de Huelva

Jamón de teruel

Italy
Prosciutto di Carpegna

Prosciutto di Modena

Prosciutto di Parma

Prosciutto di San Daniele

Prosciutto di Veneto Berico-Euganeo

Prosciutto Toscano

Valle d'Aosta Jambon de Bosses

Valle d'Aosta Lard d'Arnad

Speck dell'Alto Adige

Portugal
Presunto de Barrancos

IGP

Protected geographical indication

Ham linked to a regional area at one stage of production, development or maturing.

Germany
Ammerländer-Dielenrauchschinken-Katenschinken

Ammerländer-Schinken-Knochenschinken

Schwarzwälder Schinken

Austria
Tiroler Speck

Belgium
Ardennes ham

France
Bayonne ham

Ardennes ham

Italy
Prosciutto di Norcia

Portugal
Presunto de Barroso

STG

Traditional speciality

Ham made in a traditional manner (development, rearing of the pig).

Spain
Serrano

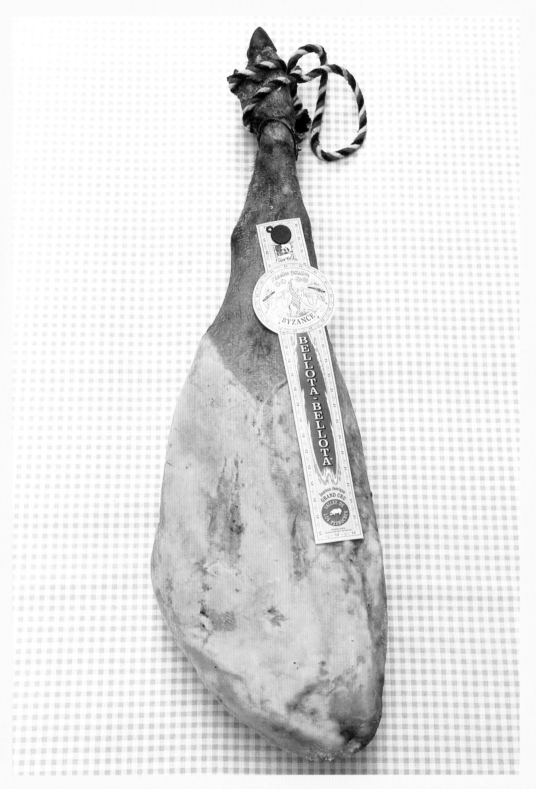

Iberico de Bellota

Ham recipes

Parma ham, rocket and Parmesan crostini

PREPARATION TIME: 20 MINUTES

MAKES 10

6–7 tablespoons olive oil
10 slices of day-old pain de campagne or rustic bread
1 bunch of rocket
50 g (2 oz) Parmesan cheese
5 very thin slices of Parma ham or other dry-cured ham,
    halved lengthways
coarsely ground black pepper

Heat half the oil in a frying pan. Add the bread, in batches, and fry on both sides until golden, adding more oil as necessary. Drain well on kitchen paper. Place the rocket in a bowl and drizzle with a little oil. Using a vegetable peeler, cut the Parmesan into shavings.

Place a half slice of ham on a board, top with a little rocket and Parmesan, season with pepper and roll up like a tortilla wrap. Repeat with the remaining ham, rocket and Parmesan. Arrange the wraps on the fried bread and serve.

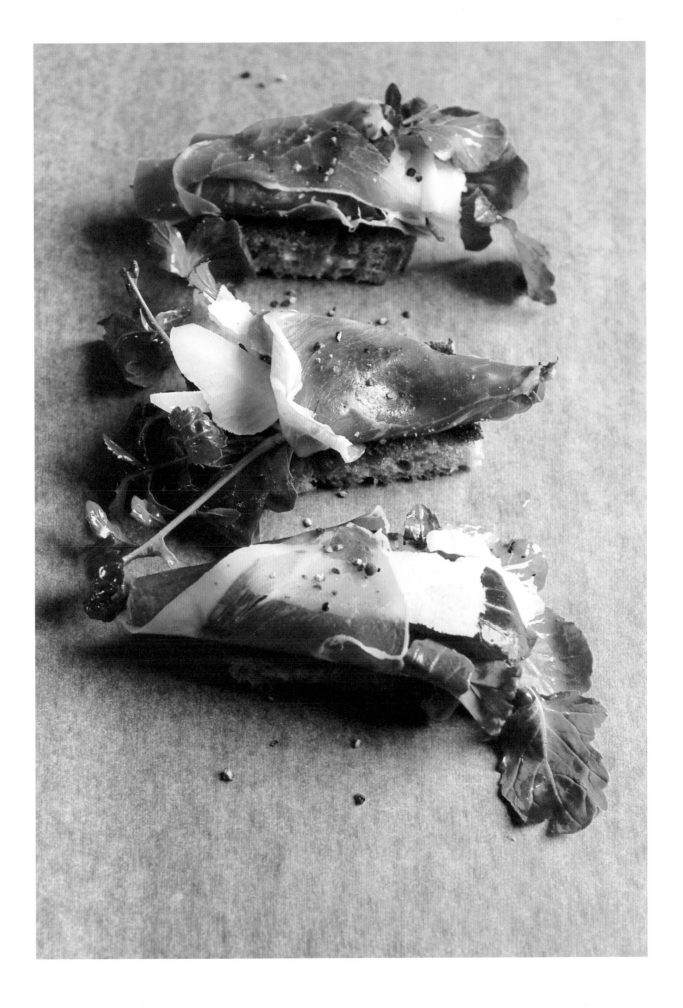

Bayonne ham with grilled pine nuts and piquillo peppers

PREPARATION TIME: 20 MINUTES

MAKES 10

50 g (2 oz) pine nuts
4 tablespoons olive oil
10 slices of baguette
1 bunch of fresh coriander
10 canned piquillo peppers, drained
5 thin slices of Bayonne (see pages 104 and 105)
  or other dry-cured ham, halved

Dry-fry the pine nuts in a small frying pan, stirring frequently, for about 2 minutes, until golden, then transfer to a plate. Heat the oil in a large frying pan, add the baguette slices, in batches, and fry on both sides until golden. Sprinkle them with half the coriander leaves. Stuff each piquillo pepper with pine nuts and most of the remaining coriander.

Place a piquillo pepper on each piece of fried bread, cover with a half slice of ham and sprinkle with the remaining coriander leaves.

PIQUILLO PEPPERS

Piquillo are sweet red peppers traditionally grown in northern Spain. The peppers are roasted, giving them a rich, spicy flavour, then peeled and packed in jars. You could use regular roasted small red peppers instead.

Hamming it up

Ham, Appenzeller cheese and dried apricot Crostini

PREPARATION TIME: 20 MINUTES

MAKES 10

5 ready-to-eat dried apricots, thinly sliced
20 g (¾ oz) Saint-Moret or Philadelphia cream cheese
1 teaspoon maple syrup
5 slices of wholemeal bread, halved
50 g (2 oz) Appenzeller cheese or
  other semi-hard mature cheese
5 slices of speck (see pages 105 and 106)
  or other dry-cured ham, cut into strips
coarsely ground black pepper

Mix one-third of the dried apricots with the Saint-Moret or Philadelphia and maple syrup in a bowl.

Spread this mixture thickly on one side of each half slice of bread. Using a vegetable peeler, cut thin shavings of Appenzeller or other semi-hard cheese. Sprinkle the cheese shavings, remaining dried apricots and strips of speck over the bread and season with pepper, or freshly cut chives if you prefer.

Serrano ham, Sun-dried tomato and basil crostini

PREPARATION TIME: 20 MINUTES

MAKES 10

100 g (3½ oz) sun-dried tomatoes in oil,
  drained and cut into quarters
6 tablespoons olive oil
1 bunch of fresh basil, chopped
3 garlic cloves, sliced
10 slices of baguette
5 slices of Serrano ham (see pages 105 and 106)
  or other dry-cured ham, halved

Set aside ten tomato quarters. Crush the remaining tomatoes with 1 tablespoon of the olive oil and half the chopped basil in a mortar with a pestle. If necessary, add a little of the oil from the tomato jar to make a purée. Heat the remaining olive oil in a frying pan, add the garlic and cook until crisp and golden. Add the slices of bread, in batches, and fry on both sides until golden. Remove from the pan and drain on kitchen paper.

Place a little of the tomato purée, a tomato quarter, a half slice of Serrano ham, a basil leaf and a few garlic slices on each slice of fried bread.

jambon de Paris, bacon, apple and curry Sandwiches

PREPARATION TIME: 20 MINUTES

MAKES 16

4 rashers of bacon
1 Granny Smith or other tart eating apple
1 celery stick, cut into thin batons
4 slices of jambon de Paris (see page 102)
  or other unsmoked ham, coarsely chopped
1 bunch of fresh parsley, chopped
4 pitta breads

FOR THE SAUCE

1 egg
200 ml (7 fl oz) olive oil
1 teaspoon white wine vinegar
1 teaspoon mustard
1 teaspoon clear honey
1 teaspoon curry powder

Preheat the grill, then cook the bacon, turning once, for 4–8 minutes. Cut it into small strips. Peel, core and dice the apple.

To make the sauce, beat the egg in a bowl, then whisk in the oil, 1–2 teaspoons at a time, until about a quarter of it has been absorbed. Beat in the vinegar, then continue to whisk in the oil, adding it in a steady stream. Finally, whisk in the mustard, honey and curry powder.

Stir the bacon, apple, celery, ham and parsley into the sauce. Cut each pitta bread in half and fill the pockets with the ham mixture. Cut each half in half again and serve.

jambon de Paris, fig, Comté cheese and dried fruit toasts

PREPARATION TIME: 20 MINUTES

MAKES 10

10 dried figs
1 tablespoon brown sugar
10 slices of multigrain bread
5 slices of jambon de Paris (see page 102)
  or other unsmoked ham, halved
100 g (3½ oz) mature Comté or Gruyère cheese, sliced
10 shelled hazelnuts
10 shelled almonds
20 fresh chives

Place the figs in a saucepan and add water to cover. Stir in the sugar and cook over a medium-low heat for 5 minutes. Using a slotted spoon, transfer the figs to a blender and process to a fine purée.

Toast the bread on both sides in a toaster or under a preheated grill. Spread half the fig purée on one side of each toast and top with the ham, cheese, the remaining fig purée and the nuts. Garnish with the chives.

prosciutto and grilled vegetable crostini

PREPARATION TIME: 20 MINUTES

MAKES 10

5 slices of aubergine
6 tablespoons olive oil, plus extra for brushing
2 lengthways slices of courgette
10 cherry tomatoes
10 slices of pain de campagne or other rustic bread
2 fresh thyme sprigs
5 slices of good prosciutto or other dry-cured ham,
  cut into strips
2 fresh tarragon sprigs
sea salt

Preheat the grill. Brush the aubergine slices with oil, then grill on both sides until lightly golden. Meanwhile, blanch the courgette slices in boiling water for 2 minutes, then drain and grill on both sides until lightly golden.

Heat the olive oil in a frying pan, add the tomatoes and slices of bread, in batches, and cook over a high heat until the bread is golden brown on both sides. Remove and drain the fried bread on kitchen paper. Cut all the vegetables into small pieces and sprinkle with thyme leaves.

Place the vegetables and strips of ham on the slices of fried bread. Season with sea salt and garnish with tarragon leaves.

Hamming it up

Ham and gherkin sandwiches (for Jean)

PREPARATION TIME: 10 MINUTES

MAKES 4

40 g (1½ oz) unsalted butter, softened
16 gherkins, coarsely chopped
6 fresh chives, coarsely chopped
1 baguette, cut into quarters
4 slices of ham, cut off the bone
ground black pepper

Cream the butter in a bowl, then beat in the gherkins and chives and season with pepper.

Slice each baguette quarter in half horizontally. Spread the gherkin butter on one half of each baguette quarter. Top with the ham and the other half of the baguette quarter and it is ready to eat.

This simple meal keeps the gherkins crunchy without the problem of later finding them on your lap.

Hamming it up

Ham, Emmental, pain d'épice and avocado Sandwiches

PREPARATION TIME: 10 MINUTES

MAKES 20

5 rashers of smoked bacon
10 slices of good quality pain d'épice
  or other gingerbread
1 avocado
juice of ½ lemon
5 slices jambon de Paris (see page 102)
  or other unsmoked ham, halved
100 g (3½ oz) Emmental cheese, sliced
½ red onion, sliced
salt and pepper

Preheat the grill. Cook the bacon under the grill for 2–4 minutes on each side. Toast the pain d'épice on both sides.

Peel and stone the avocado, brush it with the lemon juice and mash with a fork. Season with salt and pepper.

Cut the toasts in half diagonally and spread one side of each triangle with the avocado purée. Top with the ham, Emmental, bacon and onion slices.

PAIN D'ÉPICE

Translated as spice bread, pain d'épice can be described as a more savoury version of traditional gingerbread. In addition to ginger, it often includes all or some of the following flavours: cardamom, cloves, nutmeg and rum.

My club sandwich

PREPARATION TIME: 20 MINUTES

MAKES 4

8 rashers of bacon
8 thin slices of smoked pork belly
12 thick slices of white bread,
  preferably from a batch loaf
4 slices of jambon de Paris (see page 102)
  or other unsmoked ham, halved
4 tomatoes, thinly sliced
4 hard-boiled eggs, thinly sliced
1 cucumber, thinly sliced
1 handful of rocket

FOR THE SAUCE

1 egg
1 teaspoon mustard
1 teaspoon white wine vinegar
200 ml (7 fl oz) groundnut oil
1 tablespoon tomato ketchup
Tabasco sauce, to taste
a dash of brandy
salt and pepper

Preheat the grill. Grill the bacon and the smoked pork belly, turning once, for 5–8 minutes, until cooked through. Toast the bread.

To make the sauce, whisk together the egg, mustard and vinegar in a bowl and season with salt and pepper. Gradually whisk in the oil, then add the ketchup, a few drops of Tabasco and a dash of brandy.

Spread the sauce on a slice of toast and top with ham, tomatoes, bacon, hard-boiled egg, smoked pork belly, cucumber and rocket. Add another slice of toast and repeat the sauce and filling, then cover with a third slice of toast. Make three more sandwiches in the same way.

Secure each sandwich with four cocktail sticks and cut into four diagonally. Serve the remaining sauce on the side.

Hamming it up

Jambon de Paris, prosciutto, anchovy, tapenade and sun-dried tomato Sandwiches

PREPARATION TIME: 20 MINUTES

MAKES 10

150 g (5 oz) stoned black olives
1 garlic clove
200 ml (7 fl oz) olive oil
20 slices of white bread, preferably from a batch loaf,
    crusts removed
3 slices of jambon de Paris (see page 102)
    or other unsmoked ham, cut into strips
3 slices of prosciutto or other dry-cured ham,
    cut into strips
10 sun-dried tomatoes in oil, drained and cut into strips
1 onion, sliced and fried
10 salted anchovies

Put the olives, garlic and olive oil in a blender and process to make the tapenade.

Toast the bread in a toaster or under a preheated grill and spread the tapenade on one side of each slice.

Add the strips of jambon de Paris and prosciutto, the sun-dried tomatoes, fried onion and anchovies to half the slices. Top with the remaining slices of toast.

TAPENADE

Tapenade is a paste made from finely chopped olives, capers and anchovies. The dish comes originally from Provence and is now popular all over the Mediterranean. It is delicious both on its own, on toast, or as part of a more elaborate dish.

Fourme d'Ambert cheese quiche

PREPARATION TIME: 20 MINUTES
COOKING TIME: 30 MINUTES

SERVES 6

100 g (3½ oz) pork rind or lardons
100 g (3½ oz) lardons
3 eggs
500 ml (18 fl oz) milk
a pinch of freshly grated nutmeg
350 g (12 oz) shortcrust pastry dough,
  thawed if frozen
plain flour, for dusting
100 g (3½ oz) mature Fourme d'Ambert
  or other blue cheese, crumbled

Preheat the oven to 180°C (350°F/Gas Mark 4). Blanch the rind in a large pan of boiling water until it has softened completely. Blanch the lardons in another pan of boiling water. Drain both and slice the rind. If using 2 quantities of lardons instead of pork rind, blanch them together in one pan.

Beat the eggs with the milk in a bowl and add the nutmeg. Roll out the pastry on a lightly floured surface and use to line a 23 cm (9 inch) flan tin. Trim the edge, prick the base with a fork and place on a baking sheet. Add the crumbled cheese, sliced rind and lardons.

Pour in the egg and milk mixture and bake in the oven for 30 minutes, or until the mixture is just set.

Quiche with two kinds of ham

PREPARATION TIME: 10 MINUTES
COOKING TIME: 30 MINUTES

SERVES 6

4 eggs
150 ml (¼ pint) double cream
500 ml (18 fl oz) milk
350 g (12 oz) shortcrust pastry dough, thawed if frozen
plain flour, for dusting
175 g (6 oz) jambon de Paris (see page 102) or other unsmoked ham, diced
150 g (5 oz) mature Comté or Gruyère cheese, diced
3 slices of prosciutto or other dry-cured ham, cut into thin strips
50 g (2 oz) shelled walnuts, chopped

Preheat the oven to 180°C (350°F/Gas Mark 4). Beat the eggs with the cream and milk in a bowl.

Roll out the pastry on a lightly floured surface and use to line a 23 cm (9 inch) flan tin. Trim the edge, prick the base and place on a baking sheet. Add the diced ham, cheese, prosciutto and walnuts.

Pour in the egg mixture and bake for 30 minutes, or until the mixture is just set.

Croque Monsieur snacks (thanks Véro)

PREPARATION TIME: 15 MINUTES
COOKING TIME: 5 MINUTES

MAKES 12

250 g (9 oz) Gruyère cheese, grated
100 ml (3½ fl oz) crème fraîche
3 slices of jambon de Paris (see page 102)
  or other unsmoked ham
6 slices of white bread, preferably from a batch loaf,
  or 12 slices of baguette

It's Sunday evening and the kids are starving: here's the ideal snack for satisfying all appetites with something tasty that can be made in no time.

Preheat the grill. Mix together the Gruyère and crème fraîche in a bowl. Divide the ham between 3 slices of bread, cover with some of the Gruyère mixture and top with the remaining slices of bread. Spoon over the remaining Gruyère mixture and grill until golden and bubbling. Cut each into quarters before serving.

You can garnish your snacks with chives, onions or spices, if you like.

Hamming it up

Smoked ham focaccia

PREPARATION AND RISING TIME: 1¼ HOURS
COOKING TIME: 30 MINUTES

MAKES 1 LOAF

20 g (¾ oz) fresh yeast
250 ml (8 fl oz) lukewarm water
400 g (14 oz) plain flour
100 ml (3½ fl oz) olive oil
½ teaspoon fine salt
150 g (5 oz) smoked ham, cut into batons
sea salt and coarsely ground black pepper

Mash the yeast with half the lukewarm water to a paste in a bowl. Sift the flour into another bowl, add the remaining water, the olive oil, yeast and fine salt and mix to a springy dough, using a mixer fitted with dough hooks. Add the ham.

Shape the dough into a ball and turn out on to a board covered with greaseproof paper. Cover with a damp tea towel and leave to rise at room temperature for about 1 hour, until it has doubled in volume.

Preheat the oven to 240°C (475°F/Gas Mark 9). Shape the dough into an oval or round, place it on a baking sheet and slash the top with a knife. Sprinkle with sea salt and coarsely ground black pepper. Bake for about 30 minutes, checking frequently towards the end of the cooking time.

Hamming it up

Vegetable and basil tart with prosciutto

PREPARATION TIME: 30 MINUTES
COOKING TIME: 30 MINUTES

SERVES 6

7 tablespoons olive oil, plus extra for drizzling
2 onions, sliced
1 aubergine, sliced
2 courgettes, sliced
350 g (12 oz) flaky pastry dough, thawed if frozen
plain flour, for dusting
6–8 cherry tomatoes
4 slices of prosciutto or other dry-cured ham,
  cut into strips
1 bunch of fresh basil
sea salt

Preheat the oven to 160°C (325°F/Gas Mark 3). Heat 3 tablespoons of the olive oil in a frying pan. Add the onions and cook over a very low heat, stirring occasionally, for 10–15 minutes, until very soft but not coloured. Meanwhile, heat 3 tablespoons of the remaining olive oil in another pan. Add the aubergine and courgettes and cook, stirring occasionally, for about 5 minutes, until tender crisp.

Roll out the pastry to a round on a lightly floured surface, then transfer to a baking sheet. Cover the pastry round with the softened onions and place the aubergine and courgettes on top. Add the cherry tomatoes and strips of ham. Drizzle with olive oil and sprinkle with sea salt. Bake in the oven for 30 minutes.

Towards the end of the cooking time, heat the remaining olive oil in a small frying pan. Add the basil leaves and fry for a few minutes. Remove with a slotted spoon, sprinkle them over the tart and serve immediately.

Hamming it up

The pig goes east

THE PIG GOES EAST

EXPORTED, IMPORTED, THE PIG IS INTERNATIONAL!

Pigs from the East turn up in many different forms to please our Western palates. Eastern pork products are rich in spicy flavours and include sweet–sour varieties.

Trust the gastronomic wealth offered by the Asiatic pig and let some unlikely flavour combinations surprise you. No pig ever looks very unhappy on the Great Wall of China. And pigs are a lot of fun in the Land of the Rising Sun.

Steamed pork buns

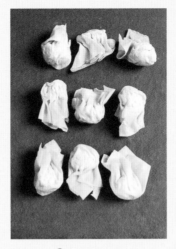

Pork wontons

Steamed pork puffs

Citronella sausages

Pork dim sum

Cooked pig's blood

Thai pork pâté

Pig's tripe

Sausage with
black mushrooms

Pâtés and terrines

Roast pork with thyme and parsley

PREPARATION TIME: 30 MINUTES
COOKING TIME: 2 HOURS

SERVES 6

1 boneless pork blade
1 pork filet mignon
3 fresh thyme sprigs
1 bunch of fresh parsley, finely chopped
5 garlic cloves, finely chopped
2 shallots, finely chopped
salt and coarsely ground black pepper

Preheat the oven to 160°C (325°F/Gas Mark 3). Trim the pork blade, then cut it into a rectangle the same length as the filet mignon. Remove the leaves from the thyme and mix with the parsley. Sprinkle the mixture over the pork blade, then sprinkle with the garlic and shallots. Season well with salt.

Place the filet mignon along one side of the pork blade, then roll up the pork tightly. Tie with kitchen string and roll in pepper.

Roast in the oven, turning frequently, for 2 hours, until highly caramelized. The roast can be eaten hot or cold.

René

LIKE MY GRANDPA BUT WITH MORE HAIR

René, now the head of the Barbe butcher's shop, is Grandpa's worthy successor. For many years he had to compromise between Grandpa, with his firm ideas of how it ought to be run, and his own sensible way of adapting to new regulations. He patiently used his expertise to make the Barbe shop into a really high-class establishment. Although he has been retired for five years now, not an extra gram of weight spoils the fit of his professional clothing, a uniform which may be short on gold braid but is worn with passionate commitment.

René's pâté

PREPARATION TIME: 30 MINUTES
COOKING TIME: 1½ HOURS
STANDING TIME: 48 HOURS

MAKES 1 kg (2¼ lb)

400 g (1 lb 8½ oz) pork belly or other fatty pork cut
600 g (11 oz) boneless pork blade
4 garlic cloves, chopped
3 shallots, chopped
100 ml (3½ fl oz) white wine
50 ml (2 fl oz) rum
100 ml (3½ fl oz) double cream
2 eggs, lightly beaten
1 teaspoon ground mixed spice
6–8 thin slices of pork or bacon fat
2 bay leaves
2 fresh thyme sprigs
salt and pepper

Preheat the oven to 180°C (350°F/Gas Mark 4). Mince all the meat with the coarse blade of a mincer or in a food processor and place in a bowl. Add the garlic, shallots, wine, rum, cream, eggs and spice, season with salt and pepper and mix well until thoroughly combined.

Line a terrine with some of the fat, fill with the prepared mixture, smooth the top and cover with the remaining fat. Place the bay leaves on top and sprinkle with the thyme leaves. Cover with the lid and place in a roasting tin. Pour enough boiling water into the tin to come about halfway up the sides of the terrine and bake in the oven for 1½ hours.

Leave the terrine to stand for 48 hours before serving.

Terrine beaujolais

PREPARATION TIME: 30 MINUTES
COOKING TIME: 2 HOURS
STANDING TIME: 3 HOURS, PLUS 48 HOURS

MAKES 1.5 kg (3¼ lb)

500 g (1 lb 2 oz) pig's liver
80 g (3 oz) smoked bacon
130 g (4½ oz) pork fat
250 g (9 oz) pork shoulder
250 g (9 oz) boneless pork blade
6 garlic cloves, chopped
2 onions, chopped
500 ml (18 fl oz) Beaujolais wine
50 ml (2 fl oz) cognac or brandy
1 teaspoon freshly grated nutmeg
100 g (3½ oz) pig's caul fat
salt and pepper

Mince all the meat with the coarse blade of a mincer or in a food processor and place in a bowl. Add the garlic, onions, wine, cognac or brandy and nutmeg, season with salt and pepper and mix well until thoroughly combined.

Fill a terrine with this mixture and cover with caul fat. Leave in the refrigerator for 3 hours. Preheat the oven to 180°C (350°F/Gas Mark 4).

Place the terrine in a roasting tin. Add boiling water to the tin to come about halfway up the sides of the terrine. Bake for 2 hours, until the top is well browned.

Leave the terrine to stand for 48 hours before serving.

Pâtés and terrines

Bibi

BISTRO OWNER OF THE NEW GENERATION

A bistro manager of the new generation, his paunch as welcoming as a soft pillow to a tired head at night, Bibi has such a tuneful accent that you need a musical ear to decode everything he says.

He wears a shirt so freshly ironed that when he starts serving guests it almost smells like the flowers of the field; by the time he's finished serving it has begun to look like a field full of flowers.

Resembling the singers Dany Brillant and Dario Moreno, Bibi had the looks for a career in show business himself, but he went in for bistro management the way other men might kiss a pretty girl – with passion and pride and that little extra something which brings customers back to his place.

Bibi's head-to-foot terrine

PREPARATION TIME: 45 MINUTES
COOKING TIME: 3 HOURS 20 MINUTES
STANDING TIME: 24 HOURS

MAKES 1.5 kg (3¼ lb)

4 pig's trotters
4 pig's cheeks
2 pig's snouts
3 pig's ears
2 pig's tongues
200 g (7 oz) pork blade
200 g (7 oz) pork belly
4 onions
4 cloves
6 carrots
2 leeks, halved
1 celeriac, cut into chunks
1 fennel bulb, cut into quarters
2 bay leaves
4 garlic cloves
salt and pepper

Put all the meat in a large pan. Stud the onions with the cloves and add to the pan with the carrots, leeks, celeriac, fennel, bay leaves and garlic. Pour in water to cover and bring to the boil, then lower the heat and simmer for 3 hours.

Remove the meat from the pan with a slotted spoon and reserve the stock. Cut the meat off the bones. Coarsely chop all the meat, place in a bowl, mix well and season with salt and pepper.

Return the pan of stock to the boil, without removing the vegetables, and cook until reduced to 1 litre (1¾ pints). Strain into a clean bowl and discard the vegetables and flavourings.

Place the meat in a terrine, cover with the reduced stock and leave to set in a cold place for 24 hours.

Pâtés and terrines

Easter ham (or parsley ham)

SOAKING TIME: 24 HOURS
PREPARATION TIME: 20 MINUTES
COOKING TIME: 3½ HOURS
STANDING TIME: 48 HOURS

SERVES 10

2 kg (4½ lb) slightly salted ham
2 onions
6 cloves
4 pig's trotters
4 carrots
2 leeks
2 celery sticks
200 g (7 oz) fresh parsley, leaves finely chopped and stalks reserved
2 fresh thyme sprigs
2 bay leaves
1.5 litres (2½ pints) Bourgogne Aligoté or Chardonnay wine
6 shallots, finely chopped
1 garlic bulb, finely chopped
coarsely ground black pepper

Soak the ham in cold water for 24 hours to remove the salt, changing the water several times.

Drain the ham, place in a large flameproof casserole, add water to cover and bring to the boil. Lower the heat and simmer for 45 minutes, then drain and rinse. Meanwhile, stud the onions with the cloves. Return the ham to the casserole and add the pig's trotters, carrots, leeks, celery, parsley stalks, onions, thyme, bay leaves and wine and season with pepper. Add sufficient water to cover the ham and bring to the boil. Lower the heat, cover and simmer for 2½ hours, until the ham is very tender.

Remove the ham from the casserole and cut it into large cubes. Bring the stock back to the boil and reduce to 1 litre (1¾ pints), then strain and leave to cool. Mix together the chopped parsley leaves, shallots and garlic in a bowl. Make alternate layers of diced ham and the parsley mixture in a terrine. If you like, you can also dice the carrots used for cooking the ham and include them. Pour in the cooled stock.

Cover and leave to set in the refrigerator for 48 hours. You can serve the Easter ham with a shallot-mustard vinaigrette as dressing.

A speciality from Burgundy, this terrine is traditionally eaten at Easter, the period when hams are taken out of the salting rooms.

pig's head and parsley pâté

PREPARATION TIME: 1 HOUR
COOKING TIME: 4¼ HOURS
STANDING TIME: 24 HOURS

MAKES 1 kg (2¼ lb)

2 onions
4 cloves
½ pig's head with tongue
300 g (11 oz) boneless pork blade
2 pig's trotters
2 turnips
2 carrots
2 leeks
3 bay leaves
1 bunch of fresh parsley, finely chopped
2 shallots, finely chopped
salt and pepper

Stud the onions with the cloves. Put the pig's head, pork blade, trotters, clove-studded onions, turnips, carrots, leeks and bay leaves in a large flameproof casserole. Add water to cover and bring to the boil. Cook for 4 hours.

Remove all the meat from the casserole with a slotted spoon. Cut the meat off the bones and mix together in a bowl. Remove the carrots and leeks from the casserole with a slotted spoon, dice and add to the meat. Season with salt and pepper and stir in the parsley and shallots.

Strain the stock into a clean pan and bring to the boil, then cook until well reduced. Remove from the heat and leave to cool.

Pile the meat mixture into a terrine, cover with cooled stock and leave to set in the refrigerator for at least 24 hours.

SOME BACKGROUND

Pig's head pâté is generally prepared with all the leftover meat from the slaughtered pig. The carcass is taken away and cooked for several hours in a beef stock with the trotters and head. The meat is then removed from the bones, mixed with a *persillade* – parsley and garlic mixture – then placed in a terrine and covered with reduced stock.

Warm pâté

PREPARATION TIME: 45 MINUTES
COOKING TIME: 45 MINUTES

SERVES 6

400 g (14 oz) jambon de Paris (see page 102)
  or other unsmoked ham, finely chopped
2 shallots, finely chopped
1 garlic clove, finely chopped
300 g (11 oz) sausagemeat
100 g (3½ oz) smoked lardons, rindless
100 ml (3½ fl oz) double cream
3 egg yolks
50 ml (2 fl oz) port
a pinch of ground ginger
a pinch of curry powder
a pinch of ground mixed spice
350 g (12 oz) shortcrust pastry dough, thawed if frozen
plain flour, for dusting
350 g (12 oz) flaky pastry dough, thawed if frozen

FOR THE SAUCE

40 g (1½ oz) unsalted butter
4 shallots, chopped
100 ml (3½ fl oz) white port
300 ml (½ pint) double cream

Preheat the oven to 160°C (325°F/Gas Mark 3). Mix together the ham, shallots, garlic, sausagemeat and lardons in a bowl. Add the cream, 2 of the egg yolks, the port and the spices.

Roll out the shortcrust pastry dough on a lightly floured surface and use to line a deep pie dish or terrine, leaving an overhang at the sides. Roll out the flaky pastry on a lightly floured surface. Fill the pie dish with the ham mixture, lightly beat the remaining egg yolk and brush the overhanging pastry with some of it. Cover with the flaky pastry and seal by pinching the sides together. Cut an opening in the top and insert a funnel of greaseproof paper to allow steam to escape during cooking. Brush the top with the remaining beaten egg yolk and bake in the oven for 45 minutes.

Meanwhile, to prepare the sauce, melt the butter in a small pan. Add the shallots and cook over a low heat, stirring occasionally, for about 8 minutes, until softened and lightly coloured. Stir in the white port and cook until reduced. Stir in the cream and heat through gently but do not allow it to boil. Serve the pâté warm, coated with the shallot cream.

Pâtés and terrines

Parfait of pig's liver and Muscatel

PREPARATION TIME: 20 MINUTES
COOKING TIME: 10 MINUTES
STANDING TIME: 2 HOURS

MAKES 10 × 100 g (3½ oz) POTS

500 g (1 lb 2 oz) pig's liver, diced
100 g (3½ oz) smoked lardons, rindless
3 shallots, finely chopped
2 garlic cloves, finely chopped
12 juniper berries, crushed
1 teaspoon sugar
4 teaspoons brandy
600 ml (1 pint) Muscatel, white port or Sauternes wine
300 g (11 oz) slightly salted butter
175 ml (6 fl oz) double cream
1 gelatine leaf
salt and pepper

Cook the liver, lardons, shallots, garlic and juniper berries in a pan over a medium heat, stirring frequently, for about 5 minutes, until evenly browned. Stir in the sugar, add the brandy and ignite. When the flames have died down, add half the wine and cook, scraping up any sediment from the base of the pan with a wooden spoon, until reduced to a syrup. Remove the pan from the heat and stir in the butter and cream. Season with salt and pepper.

Spoon the mixture into ten ramekins or other small pots, filling them no more than two-thirds full, and leave to cool.

Place the gelatine in a small bowl of water and leave to stand for 5 minutes, until softened. Meanwhile, heat the remaining wine in a pan. Remove the pan from the heat, squeeze out the gelatine and dissolve in the warm wine. Leave to cool to room temperature, then pour a layer of gelatine over the parfaits and place in the refrigerator to set.

Remove the parfaits from the refrigerator 20–30 minutes before serving with toasted rustic bread.

Plain and simple rillons

MARINATING TIME: 24 HOURS
PREPARATION TIME: 15 MINUTES
COOKING TIME: 2¼ HOURS

SERVES 4

1 kg (2¼ lb) pork belly
1½ tablespoons salt
1 teaspoon ground mixed spice
350 g (12 oz) lard
3 tablespoons sugar

Cut the meat into 5 cm (2 inch) cubes. Place them in a bowl, add the salt and spice, mix well and leave to marinate in the refrigerator for 24 hours.

Melt the lard in a large pan. Add the pork and cook over a medium heat, stirring frequently, for about 10 minutes, until lightly browned all over. Lower the heat and simmer gently for about 2 hours, until tender. Stir in the sugar and cook, stirring frequently, until the meat is caramelized.

The rillons can be eaten hot or cold.

RILLONS

Rillons are pieces of pork belly that have been cooked slowly in fat (caramelised) in a covered pot. They are often served at breakfast, or as a side dish or with fruit.

Lyonnais pork scratchings

AVAILABLE FROM ANY GOOD
PORK BUTCHER

If you're out in the Halle de Lyon food market with your fiancée, make sure you're clever enough to be invited to taste something. And make sure you're not ripped off when you take out your wallet. Don't be reluctant to pour a glass of freshly drawn Beaujolais down your throat either. 'No drinking without something to eat' – that's the motto of the people of Lyon. So treat yourself to a plate of pork scratchings the size of walnuts. You'll be licking your lips and all five fingers ... and there's no risk of indigestion as they provide good healthy food in Lyon!

Pâtés and terrines

Pork rillettes

PREPARATION TIME: 15 MINUTES
COOKING TIME: 4 HOURS

MAKES 6 × 250 g (9 oz) POTS

300 g (11 oz) pork fat or lard
500 ml (18 fl oz) dry white wine
2 onions, sliced
1 fresh rosemary sprig
1 bay leaf
1 kg (2¼ lb) boneless pork blade, diced
200 g (7 oz) smoked pork belly, diced
salt and pepper

Put the fat, white wine, onions, rosemary and bay leaf in a saucepan and heat gently until the fat has melted. Add the meat and cook over a very low heat, stirring frequently, for 3–4 hours, until the meat breaks up.

Using a slotted spoon, transfer the meat to a bowl and discard the herbs. Season the meat with salt and pepper and spoon it into six 250 g (9 oz) pots, pressing it down well. Spoon some of the melted fat over the top of each pot to cover and leave to cool.

RILLETTES

Essentially potted meat, rillettes is pork meat that has been slowly cooked in fat, shredded and pounded to a smooth paste, then mixed with enough of the cooking fat to form a paste. After cooking, the mixture is packed into a terrine or ramekin and allowed to cool. Rillettes are most commonly spread on bread or toast.

Pork confit

MARINATING TIME: 24 HOURS
PREPARATION TIME: 20 MINUTES
COOKING TIME: 2 HOURS

MAKES 6 × 500 g (1 lb 2 oz) POTS

800 g (1¾ lb) boneless pork blade
800 g (1¾ lb) pork belly
250 g (9 oz) sugar
a pinch of salt
1 teaspoon paprika
1 teaspoon dried thyme
1 bay leaf, crumbled
1 kg (2¼ lb) duck fat
500 g (1 lb 2 oz) pork fat or lard

Cut the pork blade and pork belly each into four pieces and place on a large plate. Mix together the sugar, salt, paprika, thyme and bay leaf in a bowl, then sprinkle the mixture all over the meat. Cover and leave to marinate in the refrigerator for 24 hours.

Wipe all the pieces of meat with damp kitchen paper. Melt the duck fat and pork fat or lard in a saucepan over a very low heat. Add the meat and cook gently for 2 hours, until very tender and easily pierced with a needle.

Pour a layer of fat into each of six 500 g (1 lb 2 oz) pots and leave to set. Gently lay a slice of pork blade and a piece of pork belly on top of each, then cover completely with fat. Leave to set.

CONFIT

Confit is one of the oldest ways to preserve food. It describes food that has been cooked in its own juices, to both flavour and preserve it. Sealed and stored in a cool place, confit can last for several months.

Pâtés and terrines

Pork confit tart

PREPARATION TIME: 45 MINUTES
COOKING TIME: 45 MINUTES

SERVES 8

2 tablespoons olive oil
2 onions, sliced
500 g (1 lb 2 oz) pork confit (see page 176),
  coarsely chopped
1 bunch of fresh basil, finely chopped
1 bunch of fresh chives, finely chopped
6 large potatoes, cut into thin rounds
200 ml (7 fl oz) crème fraîche
1 teaspoon ground cumin
450 g (1 lb) flaky pastry dough, thawed if frozen
plain flour, for dusting
1 egg yolk, lightly beaten
salt and pepper

Heat the olive oil in a large pan. Add the onions and cook over a low heat, stirring occasionally, for 5 minutes, until softened but not coloured. Add the confit, basil and chives and mix well.

Meanwhile, blanch the potatoes in boiling water for a few minutes, then drain and cool. Process the onion and confit mixture in a food processor until finely minced. Mix the cooled potato rounds with the crème fraîche and cumin in a bowl and season with salt and pepper. Preheat the oven to 160°C (325°F/Gas Mark 3).

Cut the pastry dough into two pieces, one slightly larger than the other. Roll out the larger piece on a lightly floured surface and use to line a pie dish. Spoon in the minced confit and cover with the potato mixture. Brush the rim of the pie with beaten egg yolk. Roll out the remaining pastry dough and use to cover the pie, pressing the edges together to seal. Brush the top with the remaining egg yolk and cut a slit to allow the steam to escape during cooking. Place on a baking sheet and bake in the oven for 45 minutes.

La Caillette

MAKES 20 SMALL SAUSAGES

1 cabbage, shredded
1 kg (2¼ lb) boneless pork shoulder,
 minced or finely chopped
500 g (1 lb 2 oz) pig's liver, minced or finely chopped
300 g (11 oz) unsmoked bacon, minced or
 finely chopped
200 g (7 oz) smoked bacon, minced or finely chopped
2 shallots, chopped
1 bunch of fresh parsley, chopped
5 garlic cloves, chopped
2 eggs
100 ml (3½ fl oz) port
pork caul fat, soaked to soften
about ½ bottle (375 ml/13 fl oz) dry white wine
salt and pepper

Preheat the oven to 160°C (325°F/Gas Mark 3).
Cook the cabbage in boiling water until tender,
then drain and dry by rolling it in a tea towel.
Place all the meat in a bowl and season with
salt and pepper. Add the shallots, parsley, garlic,
eggs, port and cabbage and mix well until
thoroughly combined.

Divide the mixture into 20 portions, each
weighing about 100 g (3½ oz) – you can make
them smaller if they are to be served as
appetizers or aperitifs. Wrap each portion
in caul fat and place in a single layer in an
ovenproof dish in which they fit snugly. Pour
in white wine to reach as far as the top.
Bake in the oven for 1½ hours.

The caillettes may be eaten hot or cold.

MAKES 20 SMALL SAUSAGES

800 g (1¾ lb) chard
olive oil
2 garlic cloves, crushed
1 kg (2¼ lb) boneless pork shoulder, minced or
 finely chopped
500 g (1 lb 2 oz) pig's liver, minced or finely chopped
500 g (1 lb 2 oz) unsmoked bacon,
 minced or finely chopped
2 shallots, chopped
1 bunch of fresh parsley, chopped
5 garlic cloves, chopped
2 eggs
100 ml (3½ fl oz) port
pork caul fat, soaked to soften
about ½ bottle (375 ml/13 fl oz) dry white wine
salt and pepper

In this version, the cabbage is replaced with
chard, considered to be more digestible. Cut
out the stems from the chard and slice them
very thinly. Blanch the stems in salted boiling
water for 10–15 minutes, then drain. Blanch the
green leaves in salted boiling water for about
5 minutes, then drain and chop. Heat the olive
oil in a frying pan. Add the chard stems and
crushed garlic and cook over a low heat, stirring
occasionally, for about 5 minutes.

Finish making the caillettes as in the recipe
on the left.

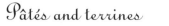

PURE POETRY

Grandpa Barbe's sausages were pure poetry for Marcou and Paulette, especially his caillettes. Representatives of the old rural tradition and loyal suppliers to my grandfather, Marcou and Paulette kept his shop stocked with pork, veal, beef and mutton for years.

An expert on caillettes, Marcou thought Grandpa's were perfection. If you hear him singing their praises, you'll feel an irresistible urge to sit down and satisfy your appetite for those delicious pork and herb sausages. Even Pavlov would find it hard to compete with Marcou when he's on form!

Pig's tongue with sorrel

PREPARATION TIME: 30 MINUTES
COOKING TIME: 45 MINUTES

SERVES 6

6 pig's tongues
2 onions
2 carrots
1 leek
800 g (1¾ lb) small potatoes, halved
3 slices of smoked pork belly, about 1 cm (½ inch) thick
2 shallots, chopped
1 small jar of sorrel preserve (see below)
175 ml (6 fl oz) Muscatel, white port or Sauternes wine
200 ml (7 fl oz) double cream

Put the tongues in a large saucepan, pour in water to cover and add the onions, carrots and leek. Bring to the boil, then lower the heat and simmer for 45 minutes. Meanwhile, parboil the potatoes in water for about 10 minutes, then drain. Cut the pork belly into large lardons. Put the lardons, shallots and potatoes in a frying pan and cook over a medium-low heat, stirring frequently, until they are well browned and the potatoes are tender.

Heat the sorrel preserve with the wine in a saucepan. Add the cream and cook until slightly reduced.

Drain the tongues and remove and discard the first layer of skin. Slice the meat.

Place a reassembled sliced tongue on each serving plate and pour the sorrel sauce over it. Serve with the potatoes.

SORREL PRESERVE

Sorrel preserve may be available from French delicatessens. If you cannot find it, use 500 g (1 lb 2 oz) fresh sorrel (or spinach). Shred it finely and sauté in 65 g (2½ oz) unsalted butter in a half-covered pan over very low heat until all traces of liquid have gone. Then proceed as in the recipe above.

Baby spinach and pig's ear salad

PREPARATION TIME: 30 MINUTES
COOKING TIME: 1¼ HOURS

SERVES 6

3 pig's ears
2 shallots, finely chopped
2.5 cm (1 inch) piece of fresh root ginger, finely chopped
1 bunch of fresh chives, chopped
100 ml (3½ fl oz) rapeseed oil
oil, for frying
1 tablespoon raspberry vinegar
400 g (14 oz) baby spinach

Cook the pig's ears in a large pan of boiling water for 1 hour, then drain and leave to cool. Mix together the shallots, ginger, chives and rapeseed oil.

Once they have cooled, thinly slice the pig's ears. Heat the oil for frying in a frying pan, add the meat and cook over a high heat, stirring frequently, for a few minutes, until evenly browned. Stir in the raspberry vinegar, scraping up any sediment from the base of the pan with a wooden spoon.

Combine the spinach with the shallot mixture and pile into a dome on individual serving plates. Sprinkle with fried pig's ears and serve.

Stuffed pig's ears

PREPARATION TIME: 20 MINUTES
COOKING TIME: 3 HOURS

SERVES 6

1 onion
2 cloves
3 carrots
1 leek
3 pig's trotters
3 pig's ears
100 g (3½ oz) pig's sweetbreads
1 courgette, diced
2 tomatoes, peeled and diced
50 g (2 oz) foie gras, diced
1 shallot, finely chopped
3 fresh chives, finely chopped
3 fresh tarragon sprigs, finely chopped
salt and pepper

FOR THE SAUCE

1 egg
300 ml (½ pint) olive oil
1 teaspoon balsamic vinegar
1 tablespoon Meaux or other grain mustard

Stud the onion with the cloves and place in a large pan with the carrots, leek and trotters. Add water to cover and bring to the boil, then lower the heat and cook for 2 hours. Add the pig's ears and simmer for a further 30 minutes. Add the sweetbreads and simmer for 30 minutes more.

Remove the pan from the heat and lift out the trotters with a slotted spoon. Cut off the meat and discard the bones. Remove the ears with a slotted spoon. Thinly slice one ear. Lift out the sweetbreads and carrots and dice both. Set the whole ears aside and mix the remaining meat, sweetbreads and carrots together.

Blanch the courgette in boiling water for 1–2 minutes, then drain and add to the meat mixture with the tomatoes, foie gras, shallot, chives and tarragon. Mix well and season with salt and pepper.

Spoon the mixture into one of the warm ears and cover with the other ear, placed the opposite way round. Roll firmly in cling film and leave in a cool place to set.

Meanwhile, make the sauce. Whisk the egg with a pinch of salt, then gradually whisk in the olive oil, 1–2 teaspoons at a time, until one quarter has been added. Whisk in the balsamic vinegar, then continue whisking in the oil, adding it in a thin, steady stream. Whisk in the mustard.

Unwrap the stuffed ears and cut into thin slices, then serve with the mustard mayonnaise.

Pig's trotters with walnut oil and caramelized onion

PREPARATION TIME: 30 MINUTES
COOKING TIME: 3¼ HOURS

SERVES 6

10 pig's trotters
200 g (7 oz) smoked bacon
5 brown onions
3 carrots
1 leek
1 bunch of fresh parsley
3 bay leaves
250 ml (8 fl oz) walnut oil
1 teaspoon brown sugar
1 tablespoon balsamic vinegar
1 red onion, sliced
1 bunch of fresh chives, chopped
sea salt and coarsely ground black pepper

Put the trotters, bacon, 2 of the brown onions, the carrots, leek, parsley and bay leaves in a large saucepan, add water to cover and bring to the boil. Lower the heat and simmer for 3 hours.

Chop 2 of the remaining brown onions. Heat 100 ml (3½ fl oz) of the walnut oil in a frying pan, add the chopped onions and cook over a very low heat, stirring occasionally, for 10 minutes, until very soft but not coloured.

Remove the trotters and bacon from the pan with a slotted spoon. Cut the meat from the trotters and chop it finely. Chop the bacon. Stir the meat and bacon into the softened onions and season with salt and pepper. Shape the mixture into sausage shapes, 3 cm (1¼ inches) in diameter, and wrap in cling film. Leave in a cool place to set.

Slice the remaining brown onion. Heat 100 ml (3½ fl oz) of the remaining oil in a frying pan, add the sliced onion and cook over a high heat, stirring frequently, for 10 minutes, until softened and golden brown. Stir in the brown sugar and cook, stirring, until the onion has caramelized.

Whisk together the rest of the oil and the balsamic vinegar in a bowl and season with salt and pepper. Preheat the grill.

Unwrap the sausage shapes and cut into 5 mm (¼ inch) thick slices. Arrange them on a flameproof dish and cook briefly under the grill until hot. Season with sea salt and coarsely ground black pepper and sprinkle with the vinaigrette. Add the caramelized onion, red onion and chives and serve.

Crunchy crépinettes with nuts

PREPARATION TIME: 20 MINUTES
COOKING TIME: 3½ HOURS

SERVES 6

6 pig's trotters
3 pig's ears
100 g (3½ oz) pork belly
6 tablespoons olive oil
3 garlic cloves, coarsely chopped
400 g (14 oz) spinach, coarse stalks removed
grated rind of 1 lemon
25 g (1 oz) coarsely chopped mixed nuts
200 g (7 oz) caul fat, soaked to soften
1 onion, grated
1 shallot, finely chopped
6 large potatoes, grated
2 eggs
1 bunch of fresh chives, chopped
150 ml (¼ pint) crème fraîche

Put the trotters, ears and pork belly in a large pan, add water to cover and bring to the boil. Lower the heat and cook for 3 hours, then drain. Cut the meat from the trotters and chop it coarsely with the ears and pork belly. Heat 3 tablespoons of the oil in a large pan. Add the garlic and cook over a low heat, stirring occasionally, until it is just beginning to colour. Add the spinach, lemon rind, mixed nuts and meat and cook, stirring occasionally, until the mixture has softened and collapsed. Form the mixture into six balls and wrap them in the caul fat. Store in the refrigerator until required – you can leave them for several days if you wish.

Mix together the onion, shallot, potato, eggs and half the chives in a bowl. Heat 2 tablespoons of the remaining oil in a frying pan and add the onion mixture, pressing it down with a spatula. Cook until the galette it is golden brown on the underside, then turn it over and cook until the second side is golden brown. (The easiest way to turn it is to place a plate over the pan and invert the two, then slide the galette back into the pan with the cooked side uppermost.) You can cook a large galette and cut it into triangles or six individual galettes). Preheat the oven to 180°C (350°F/Gas Mark 4).

Mix the crème fraîche with the remaining oil and chives. Heat a frying pan that can be transferred to the oven. Add the crépinettes and cook, turning occasionally, until evenly browned. Transfer to the oven and cook for a further for 10 minutes. Place a triangle of the large galette or a small galette on each of six serving plates. Put a crépinette on top and spoon over the chive cream. Serve immediately.

The genuine Charcutier's meatloaf

PREPARATION TIME: 30 MINUTES
COOKING TIME: 45 MINUTES

MAKES 1 LOAF

unsalted butter, for greasing
300 g (11 oz) plain flour, plus extra for dusting
4 tablespoons olive oil
3 shallots, chopped
1½ teaspoons baking powder
4 eggs, lightly beaten
100 ml (3½ fl oz) white wine
200 ml (7 fl oz) milk
100 g (3½ oz) smoked lardons, rindless, coarsely chopped
100 g (3½ oz) jambon de Paris (see page 102) or other
  unsmoked ham, coarsely chopped
100 g (3½ oz) spicy chorizo sausage, coarsely chopped
100 g (3½ oz) prosciutto or other air-cured ham,
  coarsely chopped

Preheat the oven to 160°C (325°F/Gas Mark 3). Grease a loaf tin with butter and dust with flour, tipping out any excess.

Heat 2 tablespoons of the olive oil in a frying pan. Add the shallots and cook over a low heat, stirring occasionally, for about 10 minutes, until golden brown.

Sift the flour and baking powder into a bowl, add the eggs, white wine, milk and remaining olive oil and mix well. Stir in all the meat and the shallots. Pour the mixture into the prepared tin and bake in the oven for 45 minutes.

CHARCUTERIE

The term charcuterie is used to describe both the branch of cooking devoted to cooked or processed meat products, primarily from pork, and a shop selling these products. A charcutier is the man or woman behind the counter, and they are usually a great source of information and advice on pork.

January,
somewhere in Les Landes,
the pâté team

Pompon

Stéphane

SO HOW DO YOU GET
A PÂTÉ TEAM TOGETHER?

First you need to be in luck and find the right people at the right time. In my own case, several pints of Guinness in an Irish-style pub on the eve of a Five Nations rugby match (and writing that doesn't make me feel any younger), a cigar smoked (with some difficulty) on the day of the match itself and a number of songs after the match, once again in an Irish-style pub, were a real revelation about friendship and sincerity. We would find out more about each other in the future, but it was obvious that we weren't going to split up.

Getting a good pâté-making team together calls for careful selection of the members. First you need a Jacquy, the indispensable team coach. He is the brains of the whole thing, the real boss. It is true that it's not easy to find someone like him today, but if you search the bars of Épernon carefully, you might find one. If you do, then take my advice and hang on to him. A man like Jacquy is a precious find!

And once you have a Jacquy you need a Pompon, the other star of the world of pâté. Pompon is the backbone of the organization, a veritable walking encyclopaedia on the history and origin of all good pâtés. You also need the gentle touch added to the team, in our case in the form of Kiki Pompon and Catie ... but beware, that gentle touch is only on the surface and can sometimes blaze up. (If the pâté dishes of Les Landes can't stand the heat, they should keep out of the kitchen).

If, like me, you have the luck to bring such a team together and get to know its members, you'll have many pleasures in store and will wait impatiently, like a child in front of the Christmas tree, for new pâtés to be invented. And if you just can't wait, try something else like diving with dolphins, or psychothermia (no, I'm not sure what that is either) – something with less piggy fun about it, but interesting all the same.

Kiki
Pompon

* *jacquy*

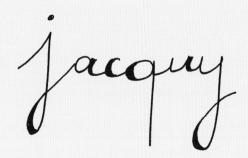

Jacquy

THE BACKBONE OF THE WHOLE THING

The backbone of the whole thing, heir to an ancestral pâté recipe, a fine organizer of happy afternoons devoted to charcuterie, Jacquy can't be caught out on the subject of the sausage. He has his own little customs and is famous for them. For instance, he cooks straight lengths of sausage laid out over a bundle of vine shoots which he always lights with the sports page of the newspaper. It seems that in the swirling smoke you can dream of wearing the blue shirt adorned with the French cockerel and of starring on a British rugby field. They say that in Podensac in the Gironde, some people apparently took it into their heads to cook rounds of sausage, and light the fire with another newspaper, just to provoke Jacquy. I suspect some malicious character bearing an old rugby-based grudge of being behind this doctrinal schism over the correct way to cook sausages. (The prime suspect is Bernard, but I say no more. We are making our enquiries.)

Be that as it may, thanks to Jacquy the tradition still goes on. Sausages are cooked as he likes them, we have more and more pâté afternoons and the distillers of Armagnac brandy needn't shut up shop just yet.

+ Catie

JACQUY'S WONDERFUL WIFE

She keeps an eye on the quantities and seasoning, she checks anything that goes too far, she tastes the mixture and gives the go-ahead to the whole recipe.

Pompon

LEARNED PROFESSOR OF PÂTÉ, WELL KNOWN IN THE SAUTERNES AREAS

Disciple of Jacquy, chameleon of the digestif

As a keen collector of fine wines and spirits, Pompon is our official Armagnac supplier. Pâté would be a wretched thing without Armagnac — and so would Pompon.

He is the festive spirit behind at least half a dozen pâtés, moderate in everything and never puts a foot wrong when it comes to celebrating an afternoon of fine charcuterie.

Kiki pompon

POMPON'S WONDERFUL WIFE

She provides the allspice and the meat mixture for the pâté, she's in charge of the evening celebrations, she can dance the fandango and lead the ensemble ... Kiki Pompon need not blush over her spices, although the spicy pâté itself may colour up.

jacquy's terrine *

PREPARATION TIME: 1 DAY OR MORE (IT ALL DEPENDS ON HOW MUCH YOUR FRIENDS HELP)
COOKING TIME: 3 HOURS (A FEW ROUNDS OF DRINKS)

MAKES 15 × 250 g (9 oz) PRESERVING JARS

2.5 kg (5½ lb) pork belly
800 g (1¾ lb) pig's liver
Jacquy (it's a good idea to have him around to make the pâté)
4 onions
8 garlic cloves
3 eggs
1 tablespoon piment d'Espelette or hot paprika
25 g (1 oz) salt
15 g (½ oz) pepper
Pompon (where Jacquy goes, Pompon goes too,
   or the other way round – I can't remember!)
100 ml (3½ fl oz) Armagnac
   (be generous to allow for tasting!)

Dice the pork belly and liver into large cubes and then mince them with a meat mincer or in a food processor. Have a drink to ward off cramp. Peel and chop the onions. Peel the garlic and remove the green shoots. Have a break and a snack to ward off any cravings. Mix the meat with the eggs, onions, garlic and piment d'Espelette in a bowl and season with the salt and pepper. Sterilize the preserving jars. Ask Pompon to rinse the jars with the Armagnac, watching him like a hawk. Finish off the Armagnac (if there's any left).

Fill all the jars, making sure that the mixture is pressed down well. Have a walk, have a breather, take a deep breath...

Seal the jars, then place them in a sterilizer or a large pan and cover them with a weight. Add enough water to reach the top of the pan and bring to the boil. Lower the heat and simmer for 3 hours, checking the level of the water occasionally to make sure that the jars are submerged.

Meanwhile, sample last season's pâtés and plan the date for the next production. Careful, as Jacquy is often unavailable!

It is better to wait a few months before eating the pâté.

* See the following pages for fuller details.

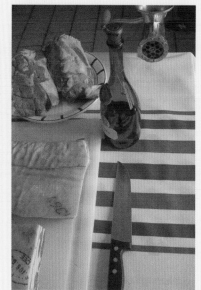

1 Dice the pork belly and the liver into large cubes and mince them both. Have a drink to ward off cramp.

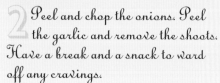

2 Peel and chop the onions. Peel the garlic and remove the shoots. Have a break and a snack to ward off any cravings.

jacquy's
terrine

3 Mix the meat with the eggs, onions, garlic and piment d'Espelette in a bowl and season with the salt and pepper. Ask Pompon to rinse the preserving jars with the Armagnac, watching him like a hawk. Finish off the Armagnac (if there's any left).

4 Fill all the jars, making sure that the mixture is pressed down well. Have a walk, have a breather, take a deep breath. . .

5 Seal the jars, then place them in a sterilizer or a large pan and cover them with a weight. Add enough water to reach the top of the pan and bring to the boil. Lower the heat and simmer for 3 hours, checking the level of the water occasionally to make sure that the jars are submerged.

During this time taste last season's pâtés and plan the date for the next production. Careful, as Jacquy is often unavailable!

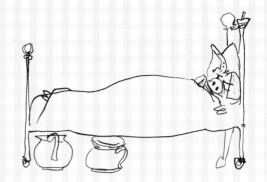

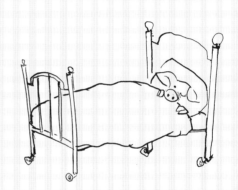

Granny pig

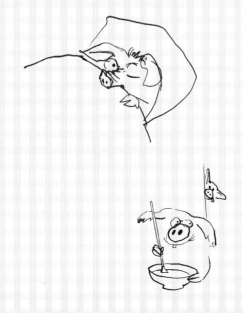

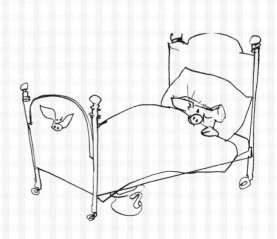

Cabbage Soup

PREPARATION TIME: 20 MINUTES
COOKING TIME: 1¼ HOURS

SERVES 6

100 ml (3½ fl oz) olive oil
1 white cabbage, cored and shredded
175 ml (6 fl oz) white wine
3 large potatoes, coarsely chopped
2 onions, coarsely chopped
a pinch of freshly grated nutmeg
6 thick slices of pork belly
3 garlic cloves, thinly sliced
200 ml (7 fl oz) double cream
salt and pepper

Heat 5 tablespoons of the oil in a large pan. Add the cabbage and cook, stirring occasionally, for a few minutes, until softened but not coloured. Add the white wine, potatoes, onions and nutmeg and pour in enough water to cover. Add the pork and bring to the boil, then lower the heat and simmer gently for about 1 hour, until the meat is tender.

Remove the meat with a slotted spoon. Transfer the soup to a blender or food processor and process until smooth. Season to taste with salt and pepper.

Heat the remaining oil in a small frying pan. Add the garlic and cook over a low heat, stirring frequently, until it is just beginning to colour. If necessary, reheat the soup.

Serve the soup hot in bowls with a swirl of cream and the garlic chips. Serve the pork belly either in the soup or separately on slices of toasted rustic bread.

Hello to Papily, who adores cabbage soup, especially when there's a lot of bacon and not much cabbage!

Hotpot

PREPARATION TIME: 30 MINUTES
COOKING TIME: 3 HOURS 10 MINUTES

SERVES 6

1 ham knuckle or hock
1 onion
1 bouquet garni
500 g (1 lb 2 oz) lightly salted pork ribs
1 Morteau sausage (see pages 64 and 65)
  or other large smoked sausage
6 saucisses paysannes (see pages 64 and 65)
  or other country-style sausages
1 piece of smoked bacon
1 cabbage, cored and cut into 6 pieces
6 carrots
6 turnip tops
6 small potatoes
1 celeriac
3 leeks, halved

Put the ham knuckle, onion and bouquet garni in a large flameproof casserole, add water to cover and bring to the boil. Lower the heat and cook for 2½ hours. Alternatively, cook in a pressure cooker for 45 minutes.

Add the ribs, both types of sausages and the bacon and cook for a further 20 minutes. Add all the vegetables and cook for 20 minutes more. Remove and discard the bouquet garni. Remove the Morteau or other large smoked sausage with a slotted spoon, cut it into six pieces and return to the casserole. Serve hot.

pork with lentils

PREPARATION TIME: 20 MINUTES
COOKING TIME: 2 HOURS

SERVES 6

1.2 kg (2½ lb) slightly salted pork blade
300 g (11 oz) Puy lentils
1 Morteau sausage (see pages 64 and 65) or other large smoked sausage
200 g (7 oz) smoked bacon
2 carrots
1 onion, studded with 1 clove
1 bouquet garni
500 ml (18 fl oz) dry white wine
200 ml (7 fl oz) double cream
salt and pepper

Remove the salt from the pork by rinsing it several times. Blanch the pork in a pan of boiling water for a few minutes, then drain. Put the lentils in a pan, add water to cover and bring to the boil, then drain and rinse. Place the lentils, pork, sausage, bacon, carrots, onion and bouquet garni in a large saucepan and add enough white wine to cover (if there is insufficient, top up with water). Bring to the boil, then lower the heat and simmer for 1½ hours.

Transfer two ladlefuls of lentils to a blender or food processor and process to a purée. Stir the purée into the cream.

Remove and discard the bouquet garni. Remove the pork, sausage and bacon from the pan and cut each into six portions. Mix the lentil cream with the rest of the lentils. Season to taste with salt and pepper and serve in bowls.

Classic pork with lentils

PREPARATION TIME: 30 MINUTES
COOKING TIME: 3 HOURS

SERVES 6

1 slightly salted pork knuckle or hock
1 smoked pork shoulder
2 bouquets garnis
1 fresh rosemary sprig
6 juniper berries
600 g (1 lb 5 oz) slightly salted pork spareribs
1 Morteau sausage (see pages 64 and 65)
  or other large smoked sausage
400 g (14 oz) Puy lentils
3 carrots, cut into cubes
3 onions, cut into cubes
175 ml (6 fl oz) dry white wine

Put the pork knuckle and shoulder, a bouquet garni, the rosemary and juniper berries in a large flameproof casserole. Add water to cover and bring to the boil, then lower the heat and simmer for 1 hour. Add the spareribs and simmer for a further 30 minutes. Add the sausage and simmer for 30 minutes more. Remove the casserole from the heat and set aside.

Put the lentils in a pan, add water to cover and bring to the boil, then drain and rinse. Return the lentils to the pan, add the remaining bouquet garni, the carrots, onions and white wine and pour in sufficient water to cover. Bring to the boil, then lower the heat and simmer for 30 minutes.

Remove the meat from the casserole and slice. Drain the lentil mixture and discard the bouquet garni. Put the meat and lentil mixture in a pan, add two ladlefuls of the meat cooking liquid and simmer gently for 15 minutes. Serve hot.

Grandma Barbe's Roast pork

PREPARATION TIME: 15 MINUTES
COOKING TIME: 2 HOURS

SERVES 6

6 tablespoons olive oil
1 pork fillet, weighing about 1.2 kg (2½ lb)
12 baby onions
500 g (1 lb 2 oz) carrots
500 ml (18 fl oz) dry white wine
1 kg (2¼ lb) Charlotte or other waxy potatoes, halved
50 g (2 oz) unsalted butter
1 bouquet garni
3 garlic cloves
1 bunch of fresh parsley
sea salt

Heat the olive oil a flameproof casserole. Add the pork and cook over a medium heat, turning occasionally, for 8–10 minutes, until golden brown all over. Lower the heat, cover and cook, turning occasionally, for 1½ hours.

Peel the onions and cut off the tops. Peel the carrots and cut the ends at an angle.

Pour the white wine into the casserole and add the onions, carrots, potatoes, butter and bouquet garni. Replace the lid and simmer for about 30 minutes, until the potatoes are tender.

Meanwhile, coarsely chop the garlic and parsley together.

Remove the bouquet garni from the casserole and discard. Season the roast with sea salt and sprinkle the garlic and parsley mixture on the potatoes before serving.

Larded and studded roast

PREPARATION TIME: 15 MINUTES
COOKING TIME: 1¾ HOURS

SERVES 6

6 garlic cloves
1 pork fillet, weighing about 1.2 kg (2½ lb)
50 g (2 oz) unsalted butter, chilled and cut into thin sticks
3 fresh rosemary sprigs, cut into small pieces
10 thin slices of pork belly
kitchen string

Preheat the oven to 120°C (250°F/Gas Mark ½). Peel the garlic and cut each clove into four. Make small incisions in the pork fillet with a small sharp knife. Insert the sticks of butter, garlic slices and pieces of rosemary in the cuts. Wrap up the pork fillet in the slices of pork belly, tying them in place with kitchen string.

Place the rolled pork in a roasting tin and cook over a medium heat, turning occasionally, for about 10 minutes, until evenly browned. Sprinkle any remaining rosemary on top, then transfer to the oven and roast, basting frequently, for 1½ hours.

Pork chops with shallots

PREPARATION TIME: 5 MINUTES
COOKING TIME: 20 MINUTES

SERVES 6

50 g (2 oz) unsalted butter
8 shallots, chopped
6 pork chops
10 fresh thyme sprigs, preferably in flower
sea salt
coarsely ground black pepper

Melt 20 g (¾ oz) of the butter in a pan. Add the shallots and cook, stirring frequently, over a high heat for 8–10 minutes, until golden brown.

Melt the remaining butter in a frying pan. Add the chops and cook over a high heat for 5 minutes on each side, or until cooked through and the juices have caramelized.

Season with sea salt and coarsely ground black pepper. Mix the thyme with the shallots. Serve the chops immediately with the shallots.

Pork shoulder with milk

PREPARATION TIME: 5 MINUTES
COOKING TIME: 2 HOURS

SERVES 6

1 pork shoulder, weighing about 1.5 kg (3¼ lb)
2 litres (3½ pints) milk
3 garlic cloves
1 fresh thyme sprig
1 fresh rosemary sprig
2 bay leaves

Preheat the oven to 180°C (350°F/Gas Mark 4). Put the pork in a large casserole, pour in the milk and add the garlic, thyme, rosemary and bay leaves.

Cover the casserole and bake, for about 2 hours, until the milk has almost completely evaporated. Discard the herbs. The pork may be eaten cold or hot, served with the milk 'jam' taken from the base of the casserole.

Roast rack of piglet with polenta chips

PREPARATION TIME: 1 HOUR
COOKING TIME: 1 HOUR 25 MINUTES

SERVES 6

1 litre (1¾ pints) milk
200 g (7 oz) polenta
4 eggs, lightly beaten
6 tablespoons olive oil
1 rack of 6 chops from a piglet
2 lemongrass stalks, coarsely chopped
6 garlic cloves, coarsely chopped
3 shallots, coarsely chopped
5 cm (2 inch) piece of fresh root ginger, coarsely chopped
1 fresh thyme sprig
175 ml (6 fl oz) white wine
50 g (2 oz) unsalted butter

Pour the milk into a pan and bring to the boil. Add the polenta in a steady stream and cook over a low heat, stirring constantly, until the polenta comes away from the sides of the pan. This will take 20–30 minutes for ordinary polenta and about 5 minutes for quick-cook polenta. Stir in the eggs and cook for a further 10 minutes. Spread out the polenta in a layer about 1 cm (½ inch) thick on a sheet of greaseproof paper and chill in the refrigerator until set.

Preheat the oven to 160°C (325°F/Gas Mark 3).

Heat the olive oil in a roasting tin, add the rack of chops and cook over a medium heat, turning occasionally, for about 10 minutes, until golden brown all over. Add the lemongrass, garlic, shallots, ginger and thyme and pour in the wine. Transfer to the oven and roast, basting frequently, for 1¼ hours.

Cut thick chips from the polenta. Melt the butter in a frying pan, add the polenta chips and cook over a low heat, turning occasionally, until golden brown.

Transfer the rack to a serving dish, surround with the polenta chips and serve immediately.

Rack of pork with cider and apple butter

PREPARATION TIME: 15 MINUTES
COOKING TIME: 1½ HOURS

SERVES 6

1 rack of pork with 6 chops
500 ml (18 fl oz) dry cider
6 Granny Smith or other tart eating apples
3 onions, sliced
a pinch of ground cinnamon
a pinch of ground ginger
100 g (3½ oz) unsalted butter, chilled

Cook the rack in a flameproof casserole over a medium heat, turning occasionally, until golden brown all over. Baste with a little of the cider, lower the heat, cover and cook for 1 hour, basting frequently with more cider.

Peel, core and quarter the apples. Add them to the casserole with the onions, the remaining cider and the spices and cook over low heat for a further 5–10 minutes, until the apples and onions have softened.

Remove the rack from the casserole, tent with foil and leave to stand for 10 minutes. Add the butter to the casserole and beat it into the apple mixture. Cut the rack into separate chops and serve with the cider and apple butter.

Whole ham with honey and cloves

SOAKING AND MARINATING TIME: 24 HOURS
PREPARATION TIME: 30 MINUTES
COOKING TIME: 1 HOUR PER 1 KG HAM, PLUS 1 HOUR

SERVES MANY HUNGRY PEOPLE

1 slightly salted ham
4 carrots
1 leek, green part only
3 onions
2 fresh thyme sprigs
2 bay leaves
20 cloves
50 g (2 oz) unsalted butter

FOR THE MARINADE

2 tablespoons ground mixed spice
2 tablespoons curry powder
4 tablespoons sugar
2 tablespoons clear honey
2 tablespoons olive oil
½ bottle (375 ml/13 fl oz) Côtes du Rhône
  or Shiraz wine
100 ml (3½ fl oz) cognac or brandy
200 ml (7 fl oz) port

Make a note of the weight of the ham. Place the ham in a large bowl, add water to cover and leave to soak during the day before you intend to cook it. Mix together all the ingredients for the marinade in a non-metallic dish. Drain the ham, pat dry with kitchen paper and add to the marinade, turning to coat. Cover and leave to marinate overnight.

Next day, put the carrots, leek, onions, thyme and bay leaves in a large saucepan. Drain the ham, reserving the marinade. Add the ham to the pan, pour in water to cover and bring to the boil, then lower the heat and simmer gently, allowing 1 hour per 1 kg (2¼ lb).

Preheat the oven to 180°C (350°F/Gas Mark 4). Drain the ham, cut a crisscross pattern in the skin and stud it with the cloves. Place the ham in a roasting tin, pour the reserved marinade over it and roast, basting frequently, for 1 hour, until golden.

Remove the ham from the roasting tin. Place the tin over a low heat and beat in the butter. Pour the sauce into a sauceboat and serve with the ham.

Slow-cooked Knuckle of ham with red cabbage

PREPARATION TIME: 20 MINUTES
COOKING TIME: 3 HOURS

SERVES 6

4 tablespoons olive oil
2 onions, sliced
1 lemongrass stalk, sliced
2 garlic cloves, chopped
100 g (3½ oz) smoked lardons
100 g (3½ oz) spicy chorizo sausage, cut into thin batons
1 red cabbage, about 1 kg (2¼ lb), cored and sliced
1 litre (1¾ pints) white wine
2 ham knuckles or hocks
1 tablespoon brown sugar
1 teaspoon ground cumin

Heat the oil in a large saucepan. Add the onions, lemongrass, garlic, lardons and chorizo and cook over a low heat, stirring occasionally, for about 10 minutes, until golden brown. Stir in the red cabbage and white wine. Place the knuckles of ham in the pan, pour in sufficient water to cover and add the sugar and cumin. Cover and cook over a low heat for about 3 hours, checking frequently that the cabbage hasn't stuck to the base of the pan and adding more water, if necessary.

When the meat is cooked – when the flesh comes away from the bone – bring the remaining cooking liquid to the boil and cook until it has evaporated. Serve the knuckles of ham whole, covered with the red cabbage.

Glazed pork Knuckles with warm potato salad and Sarrassou cheese

PREPARATION TIME: 3 HOURS 20 MINUTES
MARINATING TIME: 12 HOURS
COOKING TIME: 20 MINUTES

SERVES 6

2 pork knuckles or hocks
1 tablespoon soy sauce
1 tablespoon brown sugar
1 tablespoon tomato ketchup
3 tablespoons vegetable oil
10 potatoes
1 bunch of fresh chives, chopped
2 shallots, chopped
250 g (9 oz) Sarrassou cheese or cream cheese
  with 40% fat
1 teaspoon chestnut or other clear honey
2 tablespoons rapeseed oil
salt

The day before you intend to serve, put the pork knuckles in a large saucepan, add water to cover and bring to the boil. Lower the heat and simmer for 3 hours, until very tender. Drain well.

Mix together the soy sauce, sugar, ketchup and vegetable oil in a bowl. Brush the pork knuckles all over with this marinade and leave to stand in a cool place for 12 hours.

The next day preheat the oven to 180°C (350°F/Gas Mark 4). Cook the potatoes in a pan of salted boiling water for about 20 minutes, until tender but still firm. Meanwhile, mix together the chives, shallots, cheese, honey and rapeseed oil.

Place the pork knuckles in a roasting tin and spoon the marinade over them. Roast, basting frequently with the marinade, for 20 minutes, until heated through and golden brown.

Place the glazed pork knuckles on a serving plate. Drain the potatoes, cut into rounds and spoon the cheese mixture over them. Serve immediately.

Stuffed cabbage

PREPARATION TIME: 20 MINUTES
COOKING TIME: 2¼ HOURS

SERVES 6

1 Savoy cabbage
6 tablespoons olive oil
2 shallots, chopped
2 garlic cloves, chopped
100 g (3½ oz) chestnut mushrooms, chopped
100 g (3½ oz) preserved chestnuts, chopped
200 g (7 oz) cooked pork, chopped
250 g (9 oz) sausagemeat
20 g (¾ oz) unsalted butter
175 ml (6 fl oz) white wine
salt and pepper

Core the cabbage and separate the leaves. Select 12 large leaves, blanch them in salted boiling water for 1 minute, then drain and refresh in cold water.

Chop the remaining cabbage leaves. Heat the oil in a large pan. Add the shallots, garlic, mushrooms, chestnuts and chopped cabbage and cook over a low heat, stirring occasionally, for 5–10 minutes, until softened. Mix together the pork and sausagemeat in a bowl and stir in the cabbage mixture. Season with salt and pepper.

Reassemble the cabbage, alternating the stuffing and leaves, and place it in a large lidded flameproof casserole or earthenware pot. Add water to the pot to come to a depth of 2 inches, and cover with the lid. Cook the cabbage in the oven for 1½ hours, adding water as necessary during cooking. Drain the cooking water, then add the butter and pour the white wine over. Bring to the boil on the stovetop, then lower the heat, cover and simmer, basting frequently, for 30 minutes.

Alsace pork stew

PREPARATION TIME: 20 MINUTES
MARINATING TIME: 12 HOURS
COOKING TIME: 3 HOURS

SERVES 6

2 pig's trotters, cooked
600 g (1 lb 5 oz) boneless slightly salted pork blade,
  cut into cubes
600 g (1 lb 5 oz) slightly salted pork spareribs, separated
300 g (11 oz) smoked pork belly, cut into cubes
2 carrots, thinly sliced
2 garlic cloves, chopped
2 shallots, chopped
2 celery sticks, thinly sliced
500 ml (18 fl oz) Riesling wine
50 g (2 oz) lard
1 kg (2¼ lb) potatoes, thickly sliced
500 g (1 lb 2 oz) onions, thickly sliced
150 g (5 oz) plain flour

Remove the meat from the bones of the trotters and cut into cubes. Put all the meat, the carrots, garlic, shallots, celery and wine in a large dish and mix well. Leave to marinate in a cool place for 12 hours.

Preheat the oven to 200°C (400°F/Gas Mark 6). Grease a lidded earthenware casserole with the lard. Put half the potatoes in the base and cover with half the onions. Drain the meat and vegetables from the marinade and place them on top of the onions, then add the remaining onions and potatoes. Pour in the marinade.

Cover the dish or casserole with the lid. Mix the flour with water to a paste and spread it around the lid to seal. Bake for 1 hour, then lower the oven temperature to 160°C (325°F/Gas Mark 3) and cook for a further 2 hours. Serve straight from the dish, breaking the seal at the table.

Super Maxi Royale Choucroute

PREPARATION TIME: 30 MINUTES
COOKING TIME: 40 MINUTES

SERVES 6

1.5 kg (3¼ lb) cooked sauerkraut
500 ml (18 fl oz) Riesling wine
12 potatoes
small Frankfurter sausage
Montbéliard sausage (see pages 64 and 65)
  or other small smoked sausage
cumin-flavoured sausage
Strasbourg (see pages 64 and 65) or hotdog sausage
Morteau sausage (see pages 64 and 65)
  or other large smoked sausage
sausage confit
garlic-flavoured sausage
cinnamon-flavoured black pudding
smoked bacon
pork belly
pork knuckle or hock
pork ribs
slightly salted pork blade

To make a good choucroute, take one good charcutier!

Boil the potatoes in water for 20–25 minutes.

Meanwhile, preheat the sauerkraut in a sturdy flameproof casserole with the Riesling. Reheat the meat in hot water, then arrange on the sauerkraut in the casserole.

Cover and cook for a further 15 minutes. Add the cooked potatoes and serve.

CHOUCROUTE

There is no fixed recipe for Choucroute but the basic ingredients are sauerkraut, potatoes, white wine and different types of meat, including all or some of the following: sausages, salted meats, fresh meat on the bone and bacon. It can be served as a side or main dish.

Granny pig

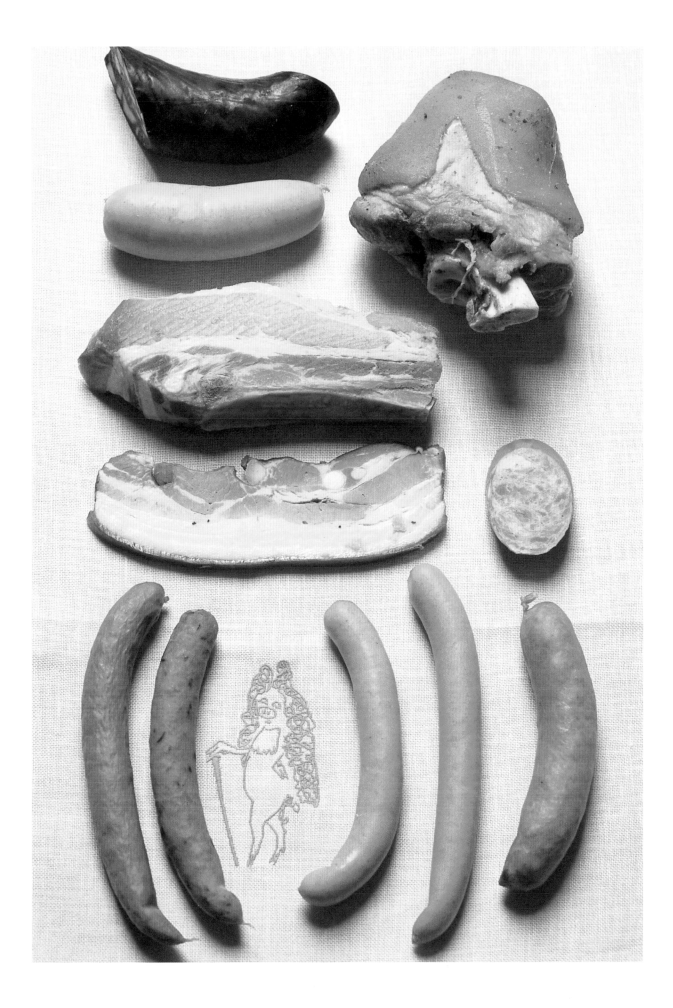

Pork ragoût with sage and brown beans

SOAKING TIME: 24 HOURS
PREPARATION TIME: 20 MINUTES
COOKING TIME: 2 HOURS

SERVES 6

500 g (1 lb 2 oz) dried brown beans,
  soaked in cold water for 24 hours
1 bouquet garni
25 g (1 oz) lard
1 kg (2¼ lb) pork fillet, cut into large cubes
2 onions, sliced
3 garlic cloves, crushed
1 tablespoon plain flour
500 ml (18 fl oz) white wine
20 fresh sage leaves
6 tomatoes, peeled
1 tablespoon tomato purée
salt and pepper

Drain the beans and place them in a saucepan. Add water to cover and bring to the boil, then drain and rinse. Return the beans to the pan, add the bouquet garni and water to cover and bring to the boil. Lower the heat and simmer for 1½ hours.

Melt the lard in a saucepan. Add the pork, onions and garlic and cook over a medium heat, stirring frequently, for about 10 minutes, until the pork is evenly browned. Stir in the flour and cook, stirring constantly, for 2 minutes, then gradually stir in the wine. Add the sage leaves, tomatoes and tomato purée and simmer for 30 minutes.

Drain the beans, reserving a little of the cooking liquid. Stir them into the meat mixture, adding the reserved cooking liquid, if necessary. Simmer for a further 30 minutes, then season to taste with salt and pepper and serve.

Spiced pork belly confit

PREPARATION TIME: 20 MINUTES
COOKING TIME: 2¼ HOURS

SERVES 6

6 pieces of pork belly, about 200 g (7 oz) each
1 litre (1¾ pints) white wine
1 tablespoon veal or beef stock powder
1 teaspoon paprika
1 teaspoon curry powder
1 teaspoon saffron threads
1 teaspoon ground ginger
1 teaspoon ground cumin
2 tablespoons brown sugar
3 garlic cloves, chopped
120 g (4 oz) unsalted butter
6 large potatoes, cut into thin rounds

Preheat the oven to 180°C (350°F/Gas Mark 4). Heat a griddle pan, add the pieces of pork and cook over a medium heat, turning occasionally, until golden brown all over. Add the white wine and stir, scraping up any sediment from the base of the pan, then transfer the mixture to an ovenproof dish.

Bring 1 litre (1¾ pints) water to the boil in a pan. Stir in the stock powder, paprika, curry powder, saffron, ginger, cumin, sugar and garlic and pour into the dish. Place in the oven and cook, basting and turning the meat frequently, for about 2 hours, until almost all the liquid has evaporated and the pork is very tender. If necessary, add more water during cooking.

Melt the butter in a non-stick pan and add the potato rounds, arranged in the form of rosettes. Cook over a high heat, turning once, until the rosettes are golden brown.

Place a slice of pork and a potato rosette on each of six plates and serve immediately.

Granny pig

Pork pot-au-feu with vegetables

PREPARATION TIME: 45 MINUTES
COOKING TIME: 1 HOUR

SERVES 6

6 slices of slightly salted pork blade
6 pieces of pork belly
3 onions
6 small leeks
6 Jerusalem artichokes
3 parsnips, halved
3 swedes or turnips, halved
6 carrot tops
6 turnip tops
1 bouquet garni
1 tablespoon vegetable oil
5 cm (2 inch) piece of fresh root ginger,
  cut into thin batons
1½ teaspoons grated or finely chopped horseradish
100 g (3½ oz) double cream
1 jar of gherkins
coarse salt

Put the meat, onions and leeks in a flameproof casserole and add enough water to cover. Bring to the boil, then lower the heat and simmer for 30 minutes.

Add the Jerusalem artichokes, parsnips, swedes or turnips, carrot tops, turnip tops and bouquet garni and cook for a further 30 minutes.

Heat the oil in a small frying pan, add the ginger and cook over a high heat, stirring constantly, for a few minutes, until golden brown. Mix together the horseradish and cream in a bowl. Place the gherkins in a serving bowl.

Place a slice of salt pork and a piece of pork belly in each of six soup plates. Divide the vegetables among them and sprinkle with the fried ginger. Serve the coarse salt, gherkins and horseradish cream separately.

Grandmother's pig's cheek bourguignon

PREPARATION TIME: 15 MINUTES
COOKING TIME: 1½ HOURS

SERVES 6

1.2 kg (2½ lb) pig's cheeks, halved
2 onions, sliced
2 garlic cloves, crushed
100 g (3½ oz) smoked lardons
2 tablespoons plain flour
1 litre (1¾ pints) Côtes du Rhône or Shiraz wine
1 bouquet garni
500 ml (18 fl oz) water
800 g (1¾ lb) carrots
50 g (2 oz) unsalted butter, chilled
salt and pepper

Heat a heavy-based flameproof casserole. Add the cheeks and cook over a medium heat, turning occasionally, until golden brown all over. Lower the heat, add the onions, garlic and lardons and cook, stirring frequently, for 5 minutes, until the onions are softened and the lardons are beginning to colour. Stir in the flour and cook, stirring constantly, for 2 minutes, then gradually stir in the red wine. Add the bouquet garni, pour in the water and bring to the boil, then simmer for 1 hour.

Peel the carrots, slice thickly at an angle then add them to the casserole. Simmer for a further 30 minutes, until the meat is tender and the sauce is thick enough to coat the back of a spoon. Season with salt and pepper.

Remove and discard the bouquet garni. Remove the meat and carrots with a slotted spoon and keep warm. If necessary, bring the sauce to the boil and reduce slightly. Beat in the chilled butter and bring to the boil, whisking constantly. Return the meat and carrots to the casserole and heat through. Serve immediately.

BOURGUIGNON

Beef bourguignon is a very well known French dish consisting of beef stewed with red wine, garlic, vegetables and a bouquet garni. The recipe above is a delicious variation.

Smoked pork shoulder with cabbage salad

PREPARATION TIME: 20 MINUTES
COOKING TIME: 1½ HOURS

SERVES 6

1 smoked pork shoulder
1 carrot
1 leek
1 onion
1 bouquet garni
100 ml (3½ fl oz) olive oil
100 ml (3½ fl oz) sunflower oil
1 egg
1 tablespoon red wine vinegar
1 tablespoon Dijon mustard
10 gherkins, diced
1 shallot, diced
1 bunch of fresh chives, thinly sliced
1 tablespoon capers
1 cabbage, cored and shredded
salt and pepper

Put the pork, carrot, leek, onion and bouquet garni in a flameproof casserole, add water to cover and bring to the boil. Lower the heat and simmer for 1½ hours.

Meanwhile, mix together the olive and sunflower oils in a jug. Beat the egg in a bowl, then gradually whisk in the oil, 1–2 teaspoons at a time, until about one-quarter has been incorporated. Whisk in the vinegar, then whisk in the remaining oil, adding it in a thin steady stream. Stir in the mustard.

Stir the gherkins, shallot, chives and capers into the mayonnaise and season with salt and pepper. Toss the cabbage in the mayonnaise.

Remove the meat from the casserole and carve into slices. Serve warm with the cabbage salad handed separately.

Pork fillet with herbs and petits pois

PREPARATION TIME: 15 MINUTES
COOKING TIME: 1¾ HOURS

SERVES 6

4 tablespoons olive oil
1 pork fillet, about 1.2 kg (2½ lb)
200 g (7 oz) smoked lardons
3 shallots, halved
4 garlic cloves, crushed
175 ml (6 fl oz) white wine
8 fresh sage leaves
2 fresh thyme sprigs
1 fresh rosemary sprig
2 bay leaves
6 baby onions
1 kg (2¼ lb) frozen petits pois
25 g (1 oz) unsalted butter
3 fresh tarragon sprigs, chopped
6 fresh basil leaves
sea salt

Heat the olive oil in a flameproof casserole. Add the pork and cook over a medium heat, turning occasionally, for 8–10 minutes, until golden brown all over.

Lower the heat, add the lardons, shallots and garlic and cook, stirring frequently, for about 10 minutes, until the shallots are softened and lightly coloured. Pour in the white wine and add the sage leaves, thyme, rosemary, bay leaves and onions. Cover and simmer, basting frequently, for 1½ hours. If the casserole seems to be drying out, add a little water.

Towards the end of the cooking time, cook the peas in salted boiling water for 5 minutes, then drain. Add the butter, tarragon and basil to the casserole and stir in the peas. Season to taste with sea salt and serve.

Roast pork with sage

PREPARATION TIME: 20 MINUTES
COOKING TIME: 2 HOURS

SERVES 6

6 tablespoons olive oil, plus extra for drizzling
1 pork fillet, about 1.2 kg (2½ lb)
1 kg (2¼ lb) large potatoes, sliced
500 g (1 lb 2 oz) onions, sliced
100 g (3½ oz) lardons
1 fresh sage sprig
500 ml (18 fl oz) dry white wine
3 bay leaves
salt and pepper

Preheat the oven to 180°C (350°F/Gas Mark 4). Heat the olive oil in a flameproof casserole, add the pork and cook over a medium heat, turning occasionally, for 8–10 minutes, until golden brown all over. Cover and roast in the oven, basting frequently, for 1 hour.

Mix together the potatoes, onions, lardons and sage leaves and season with salt and pepper. Add this mixture to the casserole and pour in the white wine. Add the bay leaves.

Re-cover the casserole and cook in the oven for a further 45 minutes, until the vegetables are tender. Drizzle with olive oil and serve.

Granny pig

Andouillettes with morels and vin jaune

PREPARATION TIME: 10 MINUTES
COOKING TIME: 30 MINUTES

SERVES 6

50 g (2 oz) dried morels or other dried mushrooms
2 tablespoons vegetable oil
1 garlic clove, chopped
3 shallots, chopped
200 ml (7 fl oz) vin jaune, an unusual wine made from
  Savagnin grapes, or other sherry-like wine
400 ml (14 fl oz) double cream
6 Troyes andouillettes (see page 66)

Put the mushrooms in a bowl, add lukewarm water to cover and leave to soak for 30 minutes, then drain. Preheat the oven to 120°C (250°F/Gas Mark ½).

Heat the oil in a frying pan. Add the garlic and shallots and cook over a low heat, stirring occasionally, for 5 minutes, until softened. Add the mushrooms and cook for a further 5 minutes. Stir in the vin jaune, scraping up any sediment from the base of the pan with a wooden spoon. Bring to the boil and allow to reduce slightly, then stir in the cream and heat through but do not allow to boil.

Place an andouillette in each of six individual porcelain gratin dishes, divide the mushroom cream among them and bake in the oven for 15 minutes, until the sausages are heated through. Serve immediately.

CLASS AAAAA

The quality of this dish depends above all on the quality of the ingredients. Ideally, use an AAAAA – Association Amicale des Amateurs d'Authentiques Andouillettes (Association of Friends for the Appreciation of Genuine Andouillettes) – Troyes andouillette, made exclusively from seasoned pork.

If the unique andouillette sausages are unavailable, another sausage of similar size can be used, but the flavour will differ slightly.

Granny pig

l'ivrogne Andouillettes

PREPARATION TIME: 10 MINUTES
COOKING TIME: 1 HOUR

SERVES 6

100 g (3½ oz) lardons
4 onions, sliced
4 teaspoons brandy
500 ml (18 fl oz) Côtes du Rhône or Shiraz wine
1 tablespoon veal or beef stock powder
20 g (¾ oz) unsalted butter
1 teaspoon plain flour
6 Troyes andouillettes (see page 66 and 258)

Preheat the oven to 120°C (250°F/Gas Mark ½). Heat a heavy-based pan, add the lardons and onions and cook over a medium heat, stirring occasionally, for about 10 minutes, until they are well browned. Add the brandy and heat for a few seconds, then ignite. When the flames have died down, stir in the wine, scraping up any sediment from the base of the pan with a wooden spoon. Bring to the boil and reduce by half.

Mix the stock powder with 500 ml (18 fl oz) hot water and add to the pan. Bring back to the boil and reduce by half. Blend the butter and flour to a paste with a fork, then beat the paste into the sauce in small pieces. Simmer for 5 minutes.

Place a sausage in each of six individual porcelain gratin dishes and divide the sauce among them.

Bake in the oven for 15 minutes, until the sausages are heated through. Serve immediately along with your favourite roasted vegetables.

If andouillette sausages are unavailable, another sausage of similar size can be used, but the flavour of this dish will differ slightly.

Granny pig

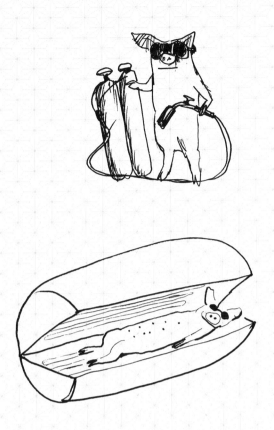

Barbecued pork

fumé

zippo

TaToo

Marinade for 6 slices of boneless pork

SPICED TOMATO

2 tablespoons tomato ketchup
2 tablespoons soy sauce
2 tablespoons lemon juice
2 tablespoons sugar
2 tablespoons vegetable oil
2 garlic cloves, crushed

LEMONGRASS AND COCONUT MILK

1 lemongrass stalk, chopped
2 garlic cloves, crushed
1 shallot, chopped
4 tablespoons coconut milk
2 tablespoons vegetable oil
1 tablespoon desiccated coconut
1 teaspoon curry powder

MUSTARD, OLIVE OIL AND OREGANO

3 tablespoons Meaux or other grain mustard
4 tablespoons olive oil
1 teaspoon dried oregano
1 teaspoon ground cumin

MAPLE SYRUP

3 tablespoons maple syrup
3 tablespoons vegetable oil
1 tablespoon white port
2 tablespoons ground hazelnuts

GINGER AND GARLIC

1 tablespoon chopped fresh root ginger
2 garlic cloves, chopped
3 fresh coriander sprigs, chopped
3 tablespoons olive oil
1 tablespoon brown sugar
2 tablespoons white wine

Barbecued pork

Crispy pork

PREPARATION TIME: 5 MINUTES
COOKING TIME: 5 MINUTES

SERVES 6

6 slices of pork belly, each 5 mm (¼ inch) thick
6 slices of smoked pork belly, each 5 mm (¼ inch) thick
spices, to taste

Roll the fresh pork belly in a mixture of spices to coat (feel free to be original when choosing which spices to use).

Cook on a barbecue grill as high as possible above the embers, as the melting fat causes flames which could burn your meat.

Barbecued pork

Breaded trotters, ears and tails with herbs

PREPARATION TIME: 5 MINUTES
COOKING TIME: 10 MINUTES

SERVES 6

6 cooked pig's tails
dried herbes de Provence, for coating
3 cooked and breaded pig's trotters, halved
3 cooked pig's ears

The trotters, ears and tails have to be cooked before grilling on the barbecue. A number of butchers sell them precooked. Packets of dried herbes de Provence, consisting of thyme, rosemary, bay leaves, basil and savory, are widely available from supermarkets, or you can make your own combination.

Roll the tails in the herbes de Provence and cook all the meat slowly on the barbecue until it is just browned.

Spareribs with barbecue sauce

PREPARATION TIME: 20 MINUTES
MARINATING TIME: 12 HOURS
COOKING TIME: 20 MINUTES PLUS 55 MINUTES THE DAY BEFORE

SERVES 6

2 kg (4½ lb) pork spareribs
200 g (7 oz) ketchup
2 tablespoons dark soy sauce
1 teaspoon brandy
2 tablespoons sugar
4 garlic cloves, chopped
2 tablespoons vegetable oil
1 teaspoon coarsely ground black pepper

Separate the ribs by cutting between them with a sharp knife. Place in a large pan, add water to cover and bring to the boil. Lower the heat and simmer for 45 minutes.

Meanwhile, mix together the ketchup, soy sauce, brandy, sugar, garlic, oil and pepper in a large bowl. Drain the ribs, refresh in cold water, pat dry and add them to bowl, turning to coat. Cover and set aside in a cool place for 12 hours.

Cook the ribs on the barbecue for 20 minutes, turning frequently and brushing with any remaining sauce, until caramelized.

Pork fillet and pepper Kebabs

PREPARATION TIME: 20 MINUTES
COOKING TIME: 15 MINUTES

SERVES 6

1 kg (2¼ lb) pork fillet
1 red pepper, halved and seeded
1 green pepper, halved and seeded
1 yellow pepper, halved and seeded
2 onions, quartered
1 tablespoon sugar
1 tablespoon balsamic vinegar
2 tablespoons olive oil
1 tablespoon ras el hanout
mixed salad leaves, to serve

Cut the pork into large 36 cubes and cut each pepper into 12 squares. Cut the onions into 36 small wedges.

Put the sugar and vinegar in a small pan and cook over a low heat, stirring until the sugar has dissolved. Pour into a bowl and stir in the olive oil and ras el hanout. Add the pork cubes, turning to coat.

Thread the pork, onions and peppers alternately on to 12 kebab skewers. (If using wooden or bamboo skewers, soak them in cold water for 30 minutes first to prevent charring.) Cook on the barbecue, turning and brushing the meat frequently with the marinade, for 12–15 minutes, until cooked through and tender. Serve with mixed salad leaves.

RAS EL HANOUT

Ras el hanout is a North African spice mix that includes cardamom, cumin, ginger, cinnamon, cloves, turmeric, coriander, nutmeg and chilli – among other spices. It is available from supermarkets and Middle Eastern stores.

Barbecued pork

Kebabs of filet mignon

PREPARATION TIME: 20 MINUTES
COOKING TIME: 30 MINUTES

SERVES 6

6 large potatoes
3 pork filets mignons
18 thin slices of smoked pork belly
18 fresh rosemary sprigs
2 shallots, chopped
10 fresh chives, chopped
150 g (5 oz) slightly salted butter, at room temperature

Prick the potatoes, wrap them individually in foil and place in the embers of the barbecue for 30 minutes.

Meanwhile, cut each filet mignon into six pieces the same size. Wrap a slice of smoked pork belly around the side of each piece and secure with a rosemary sprig. Thread three pieces of pork on each of six skewers, passing the skewers through the belly. Grill the kebabs on the barbecue, turning once or twice, for 8 minutes.

Beat the shallots and chives into the butter with a fork.

Unwrap the potatoes, cut them open and place one on each of six plates with a pork skewer. Spread plenty of shallot butter over the kebabs and the potatoes and serve.

Barbecued pork

Ash-cooked sausage with Saint Joseph wine

PREPARATION TIME: 10 MINUTES
COOKING TIME: 45 MINUTES

SERVES 6

2 large sausages
375 ml (13 fl oz) Saint-Joseph wine
2 shallots, chopped
2 fresh thyme sprigs

Make two foil parcels, each with three layers of foil, large enough to hold the sausages.
Prick the sausages with a fork, place each in a parcel and add the wine, shallots and thyme.

Seal the parcels securely and cook under the ashes of the barbecue for 45 minutes.

Cut the sausages into rounds and pour over the Saint-Joseph sauce from the parcels.

Barbecued pork

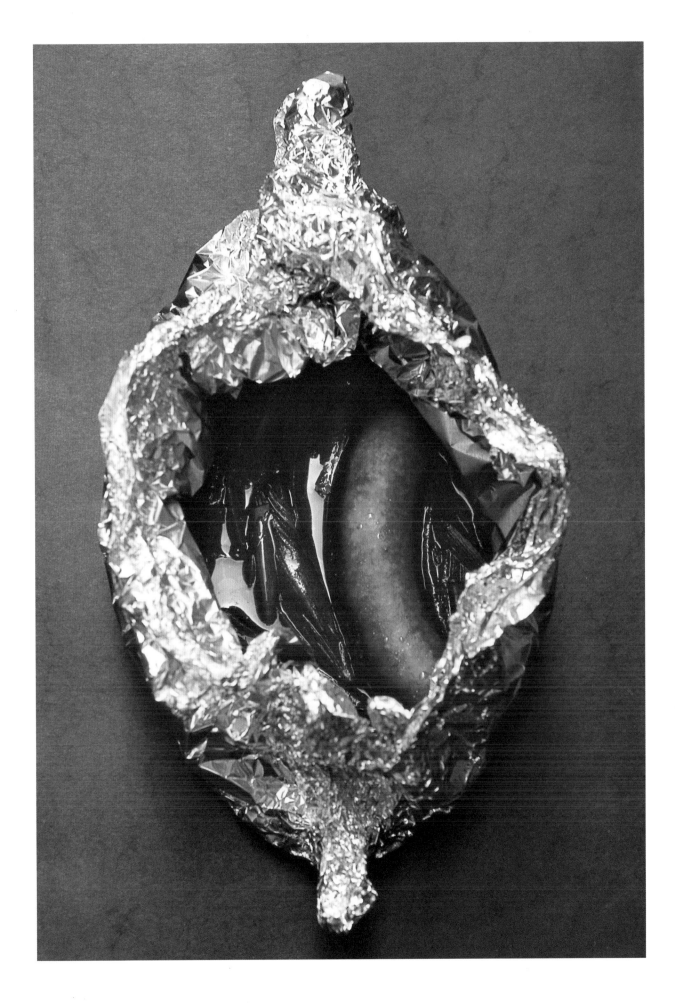

Barbecued suckling pig

PREPARATION TIME: 45 MINUTES
COOKING TIME: 3 HOURS

SERVES 12

1 suckling pig
10 shallots
10 garlic cloves
400 g (14 oz) smoked lardons
200 g (7 oz) white bread, soaked in double cream
50 g (2 oz) Dijon mustard
3 eggs
1 bunch of fresh parsley
20 fresh sage leaves
200 ml (7 fl oz) olive oil

FOR THE BASTING LIQUID

1 litre (1¾ pints) white wine
500 ml (18 fl oz) olive oil
25 g (1 oz) Dijon mustard

Ask your butcher to prepare the pig and save the liver and heart for you.

Chop all the remaining ingredients, including the liver and heart, and mix together well. Spoon the stuffing into the pig and sew up the cavity with trussing thread. Tie the trotters underneath the pig with wire and cover the ears with foil to prevent them from burning.

Whisk together all the ingredients for the basting liquid in a bowl. Place the pig on a spit over the barbecue and cook, basting frequently, for 3 hours.

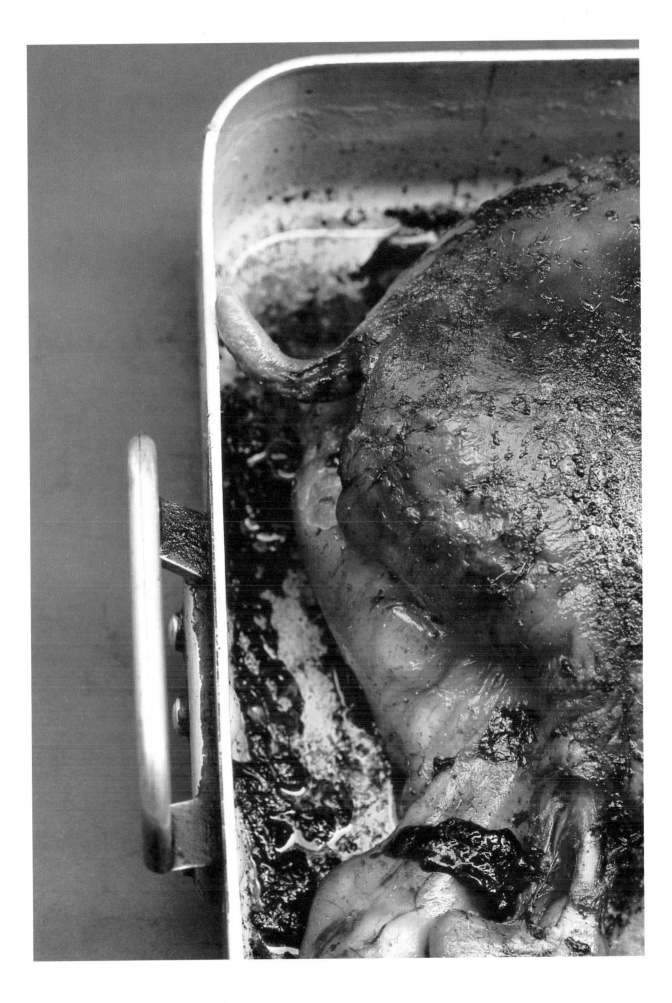

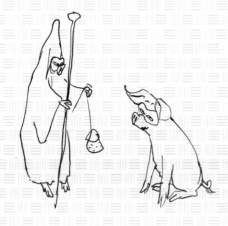

A piggy party

Celeriac cream with bacon

PREPARATION TIME: 45 MINUTES
COOKING TIME: 45 MINUTES

SERVES 6

1 slice of raw (dry-cured) ham, such as prosciutto
2 tablespoons olive oil
1 onion, chopped
1 celeriac, cut into cubes
2 large potatoes, cut into cubes
1 leek, white part only, chopped
a pinch of freshly grated nutmeg
100 ml (3½ fl oz) double cream
200 ml (7 fl oz) milk
6 thin rashers of smoked bacon

Preheat the oven to 120°C (250°F/Gas Mark ½). Place the raw ham in an ovenproof dish and dry out in the oven for 30 minutes, until crisp, then crumble and set aside.

Heat the olive oil in a large saucepan. Add the onion and cook over a low heat, stirring occasionally, for about 10 minutes, until light golden brown. Increase the heat to medium, add the celeriac, potatoes, leek and nutmeg, pour in water to cover and bring to the boil. Lower the heat and simmer for 30 minutes.

Transfer the vegetables and cooking liquid to a blender and process to a purée. Return to the pan, stir in the cream and season lightly with salt and pepper. Preheat the grill.

Transfer 200 ml (7 fl oz) of the soup to another saucepan, add the milk and heat to just below boiling point, whisking with a hand-held blender until frothy.

Grill the bacon for 2–4 minutes on each side and reheat the soup, but do not allow it to boil. Ladle the soup into serving bowls, top with the frothy mousse, sprinkle with the crumbled ham and add a slice of bacon to each.

Pork broth with sesame seeds

PREPARATION TIME: 45 MINUTES
COOKING TIME: 2¼ HOURS

SERVES 6

6 tablespoons olive oil
4 onions, thinly sliced
2 leeks, thinly sliced
6 carrots, thinly sliced
2 celery sticks, thinly sliced
1 bouquet garni
1 bunch of fresh parsley, finely chopped
2 lemongrass stalks
2 pork filet mignons, total weight about 800 g (1¾ lb)
50 g (2 oz) sesame seeds
a dash of sesame oil
1 bunch of fresh coriander

Heat 4 tablespoons of the olive oil in a large saucepan. Add the onions, leeks, carrots and celery and cook over a low heat, stirring occasionally, for 5–8 minutes, until softened. Increase the heat to medium, pour in 2 litres (3½ pints) water, add the bouquet garni, parsley and lemongrass and bring to the boil. Lower the heat and cook for about 2 hours, until the liquid has reduced by half.

Meanwhile, cut the pork into strips. Heat the remaining olive oil in a wok or frying pan, add the pork and stir-fry over a high heat for 3–5 minutes, until evenly browned. Add the sesame seeds and stir-fry for about 1 minute, until golden, then remove from the heat.

Remove the bouquet garni and lemongrass from the soup and discard. Ladle the soup and vegetables into a warm tureen, add the pork and sesame seeds and garnish with a dash of toasted sesame oil and some coriander leaves. Serve immediately.

A piggy party

Rack of pork with ginger cooked in a salt crust

PREPARATION TIME: 30 MINUTES
MARINATING TIME: 24 HOURS
COOKING TIME: 1½ HOURS

SERVES 6

100 g (3½ oz) fresh root ginger
6 garlic cloves
1 bunch of fresh parsley
3 tablespoons olive oil
1 rack of 6 pork chops
2 kg (4½ lb) coarse sea salt

Put the ginger, garlic, parsley and olive oil in a food processor and process until finely chopped and thoroughly combined.

Make small incisions in the rack at the ribs. Spread the ginger paste over the rack, wrap it in cling film and leave to marinate in the refrigerator for 24 hours.

The next day, preheat the oven to 160°C (325°F/Gas Mark 3). Spread a layer of coarse salt in an ovenproof dish, place the rack on top and cover completely with more coarse salt. You can dampen the salt slightly to make it easier to shape. Bake for 1½ hours.

A piggy party

casserole of Rack of pork in hay

PREPARATION TIME: 15 MINUTES
COOKING TIME: 1¼ HOURS

SERVES 6

1 rack of 6 pork chops, trimmed
6 garlic cloves, cut into thin sticks
4 tablespoons olive oil
3 handfuls of untreated hay
1 fresh thyme sprig
175 ml (6 fl oz) white wine
2 shallots
6 Jerusalem artichokes

Preheat the oven to 180°C (350°F/Gas Mark 4). Make small incisions in the rack with a sharp knife. Insert the sticks of garlic into the slits.

Heat the oil in a frying pan. Add the rack and cook over a high heat, turning occasionally, for about 10 minutes, until evenly browned.

Put the hay and thyme in a casserole and pour in the white wine. Place the rack, whole shallots and Jerusalem artichokes on top and cover with the lid. Cook in the oven for 1 hour. Serve straight from the casserole.

A REMINISCENCE

This recipe has something special about it because it takes me back to the end of summer, during the holidays, when the whole countryside was scented with dried grass. You are welcome to adapt it using a type of hay redolent of your past, from a farm you knew in a place you loved. And let the magic weave its spell. I myself use the hay at Gué from Marie-Cécile and Marcelou: come and smell it and you will understand why!

A piggy party

Pork filets mignons with porcini stuffing

PREPARATION TIME: 45 MINUTES
COOKING TIME: 20 MINUTES

SERVES 6

3 pork filets mignons
4 garlic cloves
1 bunch of fresh parsley
200 g (7 oz) porcini mushrooms, chopped,
  plus 6 whole large porcini mushrooms
50 g (2 oz) unsalted butter
18 thin slices of smoked pork belly
salt and pepper

Using a small, sharp knife, cut round the filet mignons in a spiral to open them up like snails. Season with salt and pepper.

Chop the garlic with the parsley. Mix the chopped mushrooms with half the garlic and parsley mixture. Melt half the butter in a frying pan, add the chopped mushroom mixture and cook over a medium-low heat, stirring occasionally, for about 5 minutes.

Spread each piece of pork with the mushroom stuffing, roll up and wrap each one in 6 slices of pork belly. Place them in a heavy-based pan and cook, turning frequently, for 15 minutes.

Melt the remaining butter in another pan. Add the whole large porcinis and the remaining garlic and parsley mixture and cook, turning occasionally, for about 8 minutes. Cut each pork parcel into six and serve with the whole mushrooms and the garlic and parsley butter.

Filets mignons in a fresh herb crust

PREPARATION TIME: 20 MINUTES
CHILLING TIME: 1 HOUR
COOKING TIME: 15 MINUTES

SERVES 6

2 aubergines, cut into large batons
2 courgettes, cut into large batons
300 g (11 oz) cherry tomatoes
6 tablespoons olive oil
3 pork filets mignons

FOR THE HERB CRUST

150 g (5 oz) unsalted butter
100 g (3½ oz) white breadcrumbs
2 fresh tarragon sprigs
2 fresh basil sprigs
2 fresh chervil sprigs
1 shallot, chopped
salt and pepper

First make the herb crust. Beat the butter in a bowl until creamy, then beat in the breadcrumbs, tarragon leaves, basil leaves, chervil leaves and shallot. Season with salt and pepper. Spread out the mixture between two sheets of greaseproof paper and chill in the refrigerator for at least 1 hour before using.

Toss the aubergines, courgettes and tomatoes in half the olive oil. Heat a ridged griddle pan, add the vegetables and cook over a low heat, turning occasionally, until tender but still firm.

Meanwhile, heat the remaining oil in a frying pan. Add the filets mignons and cook over a high heat for about 2 minutes on each side, until browned, then lower the heat and cook, turning occasionally, for 7–8 minutes, until cooked through and tender. Preheat the grill.

Transfer the pork to the pan of vegetables. Place a strip of herb crust on top of each filet mignon and grill until the crust is lightly browned. Serve immediately.

If necessary, wrap the handle of the griddle pan in foil before grilling to protect it from damage.

Pork with dates and dried apricots

PREPARATION TIME: 10 MINUTES
COOKING TIME: 1¼ HOURS

SERVES 6

1.2 kg (2½ lb) boneless pork blade
6 tablespoons olive oil
400 g (14 oz) onions, sliced
1 teaspoon ground ginger
1 teaspoon ground cinnamon
1 teaspoon ground cumin
½ teaspoon saffron threads
150 g (5 oz) dried dates
150 g (5 oz) dried apricots
6 garlic cloves, unpeeled

Preheat the oven to 160°C (325°F/Gas Mark 3). Cut the pork into even-sized pieces. Heat the olive oil in a large, flameproof casserole. Add the pork, onions, ginger, cinnamon, cumin and saffron and cook over a low heat, stirring occasionally, for 10 minutes, until the onions have softened and meat is evenly browned.

Add the dates, apricots and garlic and pour in 175 ml (6 fl oz) water. Cover and cook in the oven for 1 hour, checking frequently and adding more water if the casserole seems to be drying out.

Pork and citrus fruit with ratatouille

PREPARATION TIME: 45 MINUTES
MARINATING TIME: 2 HOURS
COOKING TIME: 1¼ HOURS

SERVES 6

1 kg (2¼ lb) pork fillet
grated rind and juice of 3 oranges
juice of 1 grapefruit
7 tablespoons olive oil
4 onions, sliced
4 garlic cloves, crushed
3 courgettes, diced
3 aubergines, diced
6 tomatoes, diced
2 bay leaves
1 fresh thyme sprig

Put the pork in a non-metallic dish. Sprinkle with the orange rind and pour the orange and grapefruit juice over it. Leave to marinate in a cool place for 2 hours.

Preheat the oven to 180°C (350°F/Gas Mark 4).

Heat 5 tablespoons of the olive oil in a large, flameproof casserole. Add the onions, garlic, courgettes, aubergines and tomatoes and cook over a low heat, stirring occasionally, for 8–10 minutes, until softened. Add the bay leaves and thyme and cook in the oven, uncovered, for 1 hour, stirring frequently.

Drain the pork, reserving the marinade. Heat the remaining olive oil in a frying pan. Add the pork and cook over a high heat, turning frequently, for about 10 minutes, until evenly browned. Transfer to an ovenproof dish and pour in the reserved marinade. Place in the oven and cook, basting frequently, for 1 hour.

Transfer the pork to a plate. Mix the ratatouille with the roasting juices, then place the pork on top. Return to the oven and cook for a further 15 minutes. Remove and slice the pork, then serve it on a bed of ratatouille.

A piggy party

Pot roast confit with lemon-flavoured coriander salad

PREPARATION TIME: 20 MINUTES
COOKING TIME: 4 HOURS

SERVES 6

2 garlic cloves, crushed
1 teaspoon coarse sea salt
1 teaspoon coarsely ground black pepper
1 teaspoon ground coriander
1.2 kg (2½ lb) boneless pork blade
1 kg (2¼ lb) goose fat
2 bay leaves
2 bunches of fresh coriander
juice of 1 lemon
2 tablespoons olive oil
1 pink grapefruit
1 preserved lemon, chopped

Mix together the garlic, salt, pepper and ground coriander in a bowl and rub the spice mixture all over the meat.

Melt the goose fat in a large, flameproof casserole. Add the pork and bay leaves and cook over a low heat for 3–4 hours. Remove the pork from the casserole and set aside, with a little fat around it, wrapped in cling film.

Pull off the leaves from the coriander stems and place in a bowl. Mix together the lemon juice and olive oil in a jug, pour the dressing over the coriander and toss lightly.

Peel the grapefruit, removing all traces of pith, and cut into segments. Discard the membranes. Coarsely chop the segments. Unwrap the pork, slice it and serve garnished with the grapefruit, preserved lemon and coriander salad.

A piggy party

Pig's cheek with fennel and olives

PREPARATION TIME: 45 MINUTES
COOKING TIME: 1 HOUR

SERVES 6

120 ml (4 fl oz) olive oil, plus extra for drizzling
18 pig's cheeks
175 ml (6 fl oz) white wine
4 garlic cloves
1 bunch of fresh curly parsley
100 g (3½ oz) stoned black Greek olives
6 ripe tomatoes
4 fennel bulbs, quartered
1 bunch of fresh flat-leaf parsley

Heat the olive oil in a flameproof casserole. Add the pig's cheeks and cook over a high heat, turning frequently, for 10 minutes until browned all over. Pour in the white wine, lower the heat, cover and simmer for 1 hour, until tender.

Preheat the oven to 160°C (325°F/Gas Mark 3).

Chop 2 of the garlic cloves with the curly parsley and 2 cloves with the olives. Cut out an opening at the stalk end of the tomatoes and stuff them with the garlic and parsley mixture and half the olive mixture. Place in an ovenproof dish, drizzle with olive oil and bake in the oven for 20 minutes.

Cook the fennel in salted boiling water for 15 minutes.

When the cheeks are tender, add the fennel and the remaining olive mixture.

Divide the pig's cheeks, fennel and olive mixture among six individual plates. Add a tomato to each and garnish with flat-leaf parsley.

 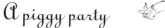

My ham and pasta shells

PREPARATION TIME: 10 MINUTES
COOKING TIME: 10 MINUTES

SERVES 6

500 g (1 lb 2 oz) pasta shells
100 g (3½ oz) lardons, cut into thin batons
2 garlic cloves, crushed
100 ml (3½ fl oz) white wine
250 ml (8 fl oz) double cream
6 slices of good-quality jambon de Paris (see page 102)
  or other unsmoked ham, cut into strips
100 g (3½ oz) Parmesan cheese, shaved
6 egg yolks
salt

Cook the pasta shells in a large pan of salted boiling water for about 10 minutes, until tender but still firm to the bite.

Meanwhile, cook the lardons and garlic in a heavy-based pan over a medium-low heat, until golden brown. Stir in the white wine, scraping up any sediment from the base of the pan. Stir in the cream and cook, stirring constantly, until slightly thickened.

Drain the pasta shells and toss in the cream, lardons and garlic sauce. Spoon a mound of pasta shells on to each of six serving plates, divide the ham strips and Parmesan shavings among them and top with an egg yolk.

Crisp filets mignons with carrots

PREPARATION TIME: 30 MINUTES
COOKING TIME: 30 MINUTES

SERVES 6

150 ml (¼ pint) olive oil
3 pork filets mignons
6 large potatoes, grated
1 bunch of fresh chives, chopped
6 eggs, lightly beaten
24 baby carrots, preferably with tops still attached
200 ml (7 fl oz) veal or beef stock
50 g (2 oz) unsalted butter
1 tablespoon brown sugar
1 bunch of fresh parsley, chopped

Heat 4 tablespoons of the olive oil in a frying pan. Add the pork and cook over a high heat, turning frequently, for about 10 minutes, until evenly browned. Remove the pan from the heat,

Mix together the grated potatoes, chives and eggs in a bowl. Roll each of the filets mignons with one-third of the potato mixture in cling film, sealing the parcels securely. Cook them in a pan of boiling water for 10 minutes.

Put the carrots in a flameproof casserole, placing them side by side in a single layer. Add enough of the veal or beef stock to cover them to a depth of 1 cm (½ inch). Add the butter and sugar. Cook over a low heat, turning frequently, for 20 minutes, until the carrots are tender and the sauce is syrupy.

Lift the filets mignons out of the water with a slotted spoon and remove and discard the cling film. Heat 4 tablespoons of the remaining olive oil in a pan, add the filets mignons and cook over a medium heat, turning frequently, until golden and crisp. Remove from the pan and drain on kitchen paper.

Mix the parsley with the remaining olive oil. Make a bed of glazed carrots on each of six serving plates. Cut the filets mignons in half and add to the plates, then sprinkle with parsley oil and serve.

Pork medallions with grilled bacon

PREPARATION TIME: 20 MINUTES
COOKING TIME: 1 HOUR

SERVES 6

18 garlic cloves
8–10 tablespoons olive oil
3 aubergines, cut lengthways into batons
12 slices of pork fillet
6 rashers of speck or bacon
175 ml (6 fl oz) white wine
50 g (2 oz) unsalted butter, chilled
salt and pepper

Place the whole garlic in a saucepan and cover with half the olive oil. Cook over a very low heat for about 40 minutes, until the garlic is tender. Remove the pan from the heat and set aside to cool, then remove the garlic with a slotted spoon and set aside. Reserve the garlic-flavoured oil.

Heat the garlic-flavoured oil in a frying pan. Add the aubergines and cook, turning occasionally, until golden brown and tender.

Meanwhile, heat the remaining olive oil in another pan. Add the pork and speck or bacon and cook over a high heat, turning occasionally, for about 5 minutes, until the pork is evenly browned. Add the white wine, bring to the boil and cook until reduced. Add half the butter and cook for a further 5 minutes, then season with salt and pepper.

Place two slices of pork and a slice of speck or bacon on each of six serving plates. Divide the aubergines and garlic among them. Add the remaining butter to the meat juice and whisk over a low heat until glossy, then spoon over the meat and serve.

A piggy party

Millefeuilles of pork and artichokes

PREPARATION TIME: 20 MINUTES
COOKING TIME: 10 MINUTES

SERVES 6

24 fresh sage leaves
100 ml (3½ fl oz) sunflower oil
4 sheets of filo pastry
1 egg, lightly beaten
6 artichoke hearts, thawed if frozen
12 slices of pork fillet
salt

Blanch 12 of the sage leaves in a pan of salted boiling water for 10 seconds, then drain and pat dry. Place them in a bowl, add the sunflower oil and set aside.

Brush both sides of the sheets of filo pastry with the beaten egg. Divide the remaining sage leaves between two of them and cover each with the remaining sheets. Cut each filo galette into 12.

Halve each artichoke heart horizontally. Heat the sage-flavoured oil in a frying pan. Add the pork and artichoke hearts and cook, turning occasionally, for about 6 minutes, until the pork is golden and cooked through and the artichoke hearts are tender but still firm to the bite. Remove from the pan and keep warm. Add the filo galettes to the pan and cook, turning once, for about 2 minutes.

Make alternate layers of filo galette, artichoke heart and pork on individual serving plates and pour the sage oil over them.

A piggy party

My stuffed vegetables

POTATOES

PREPARATION TIME: 20 MINUTES
COOKING TIME: 45 MINUTES

SERVES 6

12 Charlotte or other waxy potatoes
150 g (5 oz) smoked lardons
150 g (5 oz) sausagemeat
2 fresh thyme sprigs, chopped
300 g (11 oz) cooked roast pork, diced
150 g (5 oz) cooked lentils
1 bunch of fresh tarragon, chopped
walnut oil, for drizzling
salt and pepper

Preheat the oven to 150°C (300°F/Gas Mark 2).
Parboil the potatoes for 15 minutes, then drain.
Meanwhile, cook the lardons and sausagemeat in
a heavy-based frying pan for 10 minutes, until
evenly browned. Sprinkle with the thyme and mix
with the cooked roast pork and lentils in a bowl.
Stir in the tarragon and season.

Cut off and reserve the tops of the potatoes
and scoop out the flesh. Fill the cavities with
the pork stuffing, replace the tops, place in an
ovenproof dish and drizzle with walnut oil. Bake
in the oven, basting frequently, for 30 minutes.

TOMATOES

PREPARATION TIME: 20 MINUTES
COOKING TIME: 25 MINUTES

SERVES 6

2 slices of white bread, preferably from a batch
  loaf, crusts removed
100 ml (3½ fl oz) crème fraîche
2 tablespoons olive oil
2 garlic cloves, chopped
1 teaspoon chopped fresh root ginger
8 firm tomatoes
500 g (1 lb 2 oz) cooked roast pork, diced
1 bunch of fresh basil, chopped
2 eggs, lightly beaten
salt and pepper

Preheat the oven to 150°C (300°F/Gas Mark 2).
Tear the bread into pieces, add the crème
fraîche and leave to soak. Heat the oil, add the
garlic and ginger, stir constantly for 2 minutes,
then remove from the heat.

Finely dice 2 of the tomatoes and squeeze out
any excess liquid from the bread. Mix together
the pork, bread, basil and eggs and season. Stir
in the diced tomatoes and the garlic and ginger.
Cut off and reserve tops of the remaining
tomatoes and scoop out the flesh. Fill with the
stuffing, replace tops and place in an ovenproof
dish. Bake, basting frequently, for 20 minutes.

ONIONS

PREPARATION TIME: 20 MINUTES
COOKING TIME: 3½ HOURS

SERVES 6

2 tablespoons olive oil, plus extra for drizzling
6 large onions
1 teaspoon ground cinnamon
1 teaspoon curry powder
200 g (7 oz) sausagemeat
300 g (11 oz) cooked roast pork, diced
1 teaspoon pine nuts, toasted
1 bunch of fresh mint, chopped

Preheat the oven to 120°C (250°F/Gas Mark ½).
Place each onion on a piece of foil, drizzle with
olive oil, fold up the foil to enclose the onions
and bake for 3 hours.

Mix the spices with the sausagemeat. Heat
the oil, add the sausagemeat and pork and stir
frequently for about 10 minutes, until evenly
browned. Stir in the pine nuts and mint and
remove from the heat.

Remove the onions from the oven and increase
the temperature to 150°C (300°F/Gas Mark 2).
Unwrap the onions. Cut off the tops and reserve,
scoop out the flesh, mix with the stuffing
and fill each onion. Replace the tops, place in
an ovenproof dish and bake for 30 minutes.

A piggy party

Pork filets mignons with tomato

PREPARATION TIME: 20 MINUTES
COOKING TIME: 3 HOURS

SERVES 6

12 tomatoes, halved and seeded
5 tablespoons olive oil, plus extra for drizzling
6 large shallots
1 bunch of fresh parsley, chopped
1 garlic clove, chopped
3 pork filets mignons
sea salt

Preheat the oven to 110°C (225°F/Gas Mark ¼). Cut 24 sheets of greaseproof paper each large enough to enclose a half tomato. Place a tomato half on each sheet, drizzle with olive oil and sprinkle with sea salt. Fold up the greaseproof paper to enclose the tomato halves and bake for 3 hours.

Put the shallots in an ovenproof dish, drizzle with olive oil and cook in the oven with the tomatoes for 1 hour, until softened. Mix the parsley and garlic with 1 tablespoon of the remaining olive oil in a bowl. Cut the filets mignons into six. Heat the remaining olive oil in a pan, add the filets mignons and cook over a medium heat, turning occasionally, for 15–20 minutes, until evenly browned and cooked through. Add the parsley and garlic mixture.

Unwrap the tomatoes and divide them among six individual plates with the filets mignons and shallots. Drizzle with the garlic-flavoured pan juices and serve.

A piggy party

Shoulder of pork cooked in beer

PREPARATION TIME: 10 MINUTES
COOKING TIME: 1¾ HOURS

SERVES 6

2 tablespoons olive oil
1.2 kg (2½ lb) boneless pork blade
3 shallots, sliced
3 garlic cloves, finely chopped
2 bay leaves
100 g (3½ oz) smoked lardons
500 ml (18 fl oz) brown ale
300 g (11 oz) spätzle or fresh pasta
50 g (2 oz) unsalted butter
salt

Heat the oil in a large, flameproof casserole. Add the pork and cook over a high heat, turning frequently, for about 10 minutes, until evenly browned. Add the shallots, garlic, bay leaves and lardons, lower the heat and cook, stirring occasionally, for 10 minutes until beginning to colour. Stir in the beer, scraping up the sediment from the base of the casserole with a wooden spoon, and bring to the boil. Cover and simmer over a low heat, basting frequently, for 1¼ hours. Preheat the oven to 180°C (350°F/Gas Mark 4).

Transfer the pork to a roasting tin, baste with the cooking juices and place in the oven. Cook, basting frequently, for 15 minutes, until glazed.

Cook the spätzle or pasta in a large pan of salted boiling water until tender, then remove with a slotted spoon or drain. (The spätzle will be cooked when they rise to the surface and fresh pasta will take 2–3 minutes. Alternatively, follow the instructions on the packet.) Stir in the butter and, when that has melted, stir in the garlic, shallots and lardons together with the remaining cooking juices.

A piggy party

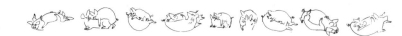

Curry

PREPARATION TIME: 30 MINUTES
COOKING TIME: 1 HOUR 35 MINUTES

SERVES 6

4 tablespoons olive oil
1.2 kg (2½ lb) boneless pork blade, cut into cubes
3 onions, sliced
2 tablespoons curry powder
1 teaspoon ground coriander
200 ml (7 fl oz) white wine
200 ml (7 fl oz) double cream
200 ml (7 fl oz) coconut milk
100 g (3½ oz) Granny Smith or other tart eating apple
100 g (3½ oz) banana
100 g (3½ oz) pineapple, cut into cubes
100 g (3½ oz) shelled almonds
1 bunch of fresh coriander, chopped

Heat the olive oil in a large, flameproof casserole. Add the pork and onions and cook over a medium heat, stirring frequently, for 8–10 minutes, until the pork is evenly browned and the onions have softened. Add the curry powder and ground coriander and cook, stirring constantly, for 2 minutes.

Stir in the white wine, scraping up any sediment from the base of the casserole with a wooden spoon, and bring to the boil. Lower the heat, cover and simmer for 45 minutes.

Stir in the cream and cook for 15 minutes, until reduced. Add half the coconut milk and simmer for a further 15 minutes. Peel and core the apple and cut into cubes. Cut the banana into chunks. Add the apple, banana, pineapple and almonds to the casserole and simmer for a further 5 minutes.

Swirl in the remaining coconut milk, sprinkle with the fresh coriander and serve.

A piggy party

Filets mignons with peanuts

PREPARATION TIME: 10 MINUTES
COOKING TIME: 30 MINUTES

SERVES 6

3 green peppers
3 yellow peppers
1 bunch of fresh coriander
2 tablespoons curry paste
2 garlic cloves
100 g (3½ oz) peanuts, chopped
200 ml (7 fl oz) coconut milk
4 tablespoons groundnut oil
3 pork filets mignons

Preheat the oven to 180°C (350°F/Gas Mark 4). Place the whole peppers on a baking sheet and roast, turning occasionally, for 20 minutes, until the skins are charred. Remove from the oven and leave to cool. Peel off the skins and set the whole peppers aside.

Chop the stems and leaves of the coriander, then mix with the curry paste, garlic and peanuts in a bowl. Alternatively, place the bunch of coriander, the curry paste and garlic in a food processor and process until finely chopped and thoroughly combined. Dry-fry this paste in a saucepan, stirring constantly, until it gives off its aroma. Stir in the coconut milk and cook until reduced.

Heat the oil in a frying pan. Add the filets mignons and cook over a high heat, turning occasionally, for 10 minutes, until evenly browned and cooked through. Meanwhile, reheat the peppers in the oven at 180°C (350°F/Gas Mark 4).

Arrange the filets mignons and the whole peppers on a board and serve the sauce separately.

A piggy party

Blanquette of pork

PREPARATION TIME: 45 MINUTES
COOKING TIME: 1¼ HOURS

SERVES 6

1 onion
2 cloves
4 tablespoons olive oil
1.2 kg (2½ lb) boneless pork blade, cut into large cubes
1 tablespoon plain flour
2 tablespoons chicken stock powder
1 bouquet garni
6 Charlotte or other waxy potatoes, diced
3 carrots, sliced
200 g (7 oz) shelled petits pois
200 g (7 oz) shelled broad beans
300 ml (½ pint) double cream
juice of 1 lemon

Stud the onion with the cloves and set aside. Heat the olive oil in a saucepan. Add the pork and cook over a high heat, stirring frequently, for about 10 minutes, until evenly browned. Lower the heat, stir in the flour and cook, stirring constantly, for 5 minutes.

Pour in enough water to cover the meat by twice its depth and add the chicken stock powder, the bouquet garni and the onion studded with cloves. Simmer, skimming the surface frequently, for 1 hour.

Meanwhile, cook the potatoes, carrots, peas and beans in salted boiling water until tender but still firm to the bite. Drain well.

Remove the meat from the saucepan with a slotted spoon. Stir the cream into the cooking liquid and cook, stirring occasionally, until reduced and smooth. Return the meat to the pan, add the vegetables and reheat. Stir in the lemon juice and serve.

BLANQUETTE

Blanquette is rich creamy stew, usually made with white meats. The meat is cooked without initial browning, and the sauce is thickened with roux and enriched with cream. Blanquette derives from the French word blanc (white).

A piggy party

Rack of pork with pepper and pissaladière

PREPARATION TIME: 45 MINUTES
COOKING TIME: 2 HOURS

SERVES 6

6 tablespoons olive oil
1 rack of 6 pork chops
6 onions, sliced
1 fresh rosemary sprig, chopped
2 fresh thyme sprigs, chopped
200 g (7 oz) bread dough
plain flour, for dusting
12 salted anchovies
20 Greek black olives
200 ml (7 fl oz) white wine
1 small can or jar of green peppercorns
200 ml (7 fl oz) double cream

Preheat the oven to 160°C (325°F/Gas Mark 3). Heat 4 tablespoons of the oil in a roasting tin. Add the rack of pork and cook over a high heat, turning frequently, for about 10 minutes, until evenly browned. Transfer the tin to the oven and roast, basting frequently, for 1¼ hours.

Heat the remaining oil in a frying pan. Add the onions, rosemary and thyme and cook over a low heat, stirring occasionally, until softened but not coloured. Remove the pan from the heat.

Roll out the bread dough on a lightly floured surface to a round like a pizza and place on a baking sheet. Cover it with the cooked onions, anchovies and half of the black olives. Leave in a warm place to rise for 30 minutes.

Remove the pork from the oven, cover with foil and leave to stand while the pissaladière is baking. Increase the oven temperature to 200°C (400°F/Gas Mark 6). Bake the pissaladière for 15 minutes.

Transfer the pork to a carving board. Set the roasting tin over a high heat and stir in the white wine, scraping up any sediment from the base of the tin. Add the green peppercorns and the remaining olives, bring to the boil and cook until reduced. Stir in the cream and cook for a further 5 minutes, but do not allow the sauce to boil.

Carve the rack, place the chops on a serving dish and spoon the sauce over them. Serve with the pissaladière.

A piggy party

Filets mignons with sauerkraut

PREPARATION TIME: 15 MINUTES
COOKING TIME: 25 MINUTES

SERVES 6

1 kg (2¼ lb) ready-made sauerkraut
175 ml (6 fl oz) Riesling wine
4 tablespoons olive oil
3 pork filets mignons
4 shallots, sliced
10 juniper berries, crushed
3 tablespoons cognac or brandy
100 ml (3½ fl oz) crème fraîche
1 bunch of fresh chives, chopped

Place the sauerkraut in a pan, add half the wine and cook over a low heat.

Heat the olive oil in a frying pan. Add the pork and cook over a high heat, turning occasionally, for about 10 minutes, until evenly browned and cooked through. Remove from the pan, set aside and keep warm.

Add the shallots and juniper berries to the same pan and cook over a low heat, stirring occasionally, for about 5 minutes, until softened. Add the cognac or brandy, heat for a few seconds, then ignite. When the flames have died down, add the remaining wine and simmer for 5 minutes. Stir in the crème fraîche and cook for a further 5 minutes.

Divide the sauerkraut among six individual plates. Slice the filets mignons, add to the plates and top with the shallot and juniper cream. Garnish with the chives and serve.

A piggy party

Pork chops with artichokes and new potatoes

PREPARATION TIME: 30 MINUTES
COOKING TIME: 20 MINUTES

SERVES 6

12 purple artichokes
800 g (1¾ lb) small new potatoes
5 tablespoons olive oil
2 garlic cloves, coarsely chopped
4 fresh parsley sprigs, coarsely chopped
50 g (2 oz) unsalted butter
6 pork chops
salt and pepper

Prepare the artichokes by peeling the stalks and removing the outer leaves. Cut off the tops of the leaves with kitchen scissors, then cut each artichoke lengthways and remove the hairy choke.

Parboil the potatoes in salted boiling water for 5 minutes, then drain.

Heat the olive oil in a frying pan. Add the artichokes and cook over a low heat, turning occasionally, until golden brown and tender. Remove from the pan and keep warm. Add the potatoes to the pan and cook, stirring occasionally, until golden brown all over. Stir in the garlic and parsley.

Meanwhile, melt the butter in another frying pan. Add the chops and cook over a medium heat for 5 minutes on each side, or until golden brown and cooked through. Season with salt and pepper.

Divide the chops, artichokes and potatoes among six individual plates, spoon the garlic and parsley cooking juices over them and serve.

A piggy party

Pork chops with Saint-Marcellin cheese

PREPARATION TIME: 20 MINUTES
COOKING TIME: 25 MINUTES

SERVES 6

400 g (14 oz) macaroni
20 g (¾ oz) unsalted butter
20 g (¾ oz) plain flour
500 ml (18 fl oz) milk
a pinch of freshly grated nutmeg
100 g (3½ oz) Vieux Comté cheese, diced
100 g (3½ oz) Gruyère cheese, grated
6 pork loin chops
olive oil, for brushing
3 mature Saint-Marcellin or other goat's cheese, halved
salt and pepper

Preheat the oven to 160°C (325°F/Gas Mark 3). Cook the macaroni in salted boiling water for 8–10 minutes, until tender but still firm to the bite, then drain. Melt the butter in a saucepan, stir in the flour and cook, stirring constantly, for 2 minutes. Gradually stir in the milk, add the nutmeg and cook, stirring constantly, for 8 minutes.

Preheat the grill. Mix together the Vieux Comté and macaroni and place in an ovenproof dish. Pour the sauce over the top and sprinkle with the grated Gruyère. Bake in the oven for 10 minutes, then season with salt and pepper.

Meanwhile, brush the chops with oil and cook under the grill for 5 minutes on each side, or until well browned and cooked through. Place half a Saint-Marcellin or other goat's cheese on each of the chops and grill until the cheese melts.

Place a cheese-covered chop on each of six individual plates, divide the macaroni among them and serve.

A piggy party

Filets mignons with Maple syrup

PREPARATION TIME: 15 MINUTES
COOKING TIME: 25 MINUTES

SERVES 6

6 rhubarb sticks, cut into short lengths
1 tablespoon brown sugar
20 g (¾ oz) unsalted butter
3 pork filets mignons
3 tablespoons white port
2 tablespoons maple syrup
1 teaspoon ground ginger
50 g (2 oz) hazelnuts, crushed
sea salt and coarsely ground black pepper

Put the rhubarb in a saucepan, add 2 tablespoons water and cook over a low heat for 5 minutes. Add the sugar and 10 g (¼ oz) of the butter and cook for a further 5 minutes, until the rhubarb is soft.

Heat the remaining butter in a frying pan. Add the pork and cook over a high heat, turning occasionally, for about 10 minutes, until golden brown and cooked through. Add the port and maple syrup and cook, basting the meat frequently, until the sauce has reduced to a syrupy texture.

Slice the filets mignons. Stir the ginger into the rhubarb, season with sea salt and coarsely ground black pepper, add the crushed hazelnuts and serve with the pork.

a piggy party

Filets mignons with pesto and crunchy vegetable salad

PREPARATION TIME: 20 MINUTES
COOKING TIME: 15 MINUTES

SERVES 6

1 bunch of fresh basil
20 g (¾ oz) pine nuts
1 garlic clove, chopped
50 g (2 oz) Parmesan cheese shavings
300 ml (½ pint) olive oil
2 carrots
2 courgettes
2 cucumbers
3 celery sticks
1 red onion, thinly sliced
1 tablespoon balsamic vinegar
3 pork filets mignons
sea salt

To make the pesto, put the basil, pine nuts and garlic in a mortar and crush to a paste with a pestle, then work in the Parmesan. Gradually add 200 ml (7 fl oz) of the olive oil, mixing well with a wooden spoon.

Using a vegetable peeler, cut the carrots, courgettes, cucumber and celery into thin strips, then slice the strips lengthways into narrow ribbons. Place the vegetable ribbons in a bowl, add the onion and mix well. Whisk together 4 tablespoons of the remaining olive oil and the balsamic vinegar in a jug, season with sea salt and add to the vegetables.

Heat the remaining olive oil in a frying pan. Add the filets mignons and cook over a high heat, turning occasionally, for 15 minutes, until well browned and cooked through.

Slice the filets mignons, place on individual serving plates and spoon the pesto over them. Divide the vegetable salad among the plates and serve immediately. This dish can also be served cold.

a piggy party

Filets mignons in sweet-and-sour sauce

PREPARATION TIME: 20 MINUTES
COOKING TIME: 15 MINUTES

SERVES 6

1 bunch of green asparagus
4 tablespoons sunflower oil
3 pork filets mignons, thinly sliced
1 cucumber, thinly sliced
2 courgettes, thinly sliced
1 red pepper, seeded and thinly sliced
1 yellow pepper, seeded and thinly sliced
1 red onion, thinly sliced
1 bunch of fresh chives, cut into 1 cm (½ inch) lengths

FOR THE SWEET-AND-SOUR SAUCE

1 red onion, chopped
2 garlic cloves, chopped
50 g (2 oz) sugar
50 g (2 oz) canned pineapple
1 tablespoon tomato ketchup
1 tablespoon wine vinegar

First make the sweet-and-sour sauce. Mix all the ingredients together in a saucepan and cook over a low heat for 5 minutes. Set aside.

Cut the asparagus into pieces and slice lengthways. Heat the sunflower oil in a wok or large frying pan. Add the pork and stir-fry over a high heat for about 5 minutes, until evenly browned. Add the asparagus, cucumber, courgettes, peppers and onion and stir-fry for 5 minutes, until tender but still crisp. Add the sweet-and-sour sauce and cook, stirring constantly, for a further 2 minutes.

Sprinkle with chives and serve immediately.

A piggy party

Tagliatelle with bacon

PREPARATION TIME: 20 MINUTES
COOKING TIME: 10 MINUTES

SERVES 6

150 g (5 oz) lardons
150 g (5 oz) smoked lardons
150 g (5 oz) chorizo sausage, cut into batons
2 garlic cloves, sliced
600 g (1 lb 5 oz) fresh tagliatelle
1 bunch of fresh basil, finely chopped
sea salt

Heat a non-stick frying pan. Add both types of lardons and the chorizo and cook over a medium heat, stirring frequently, for 5 minutes. Add the garlic and cook, stirring frequently, for a few minutes more, until golden brown.

Meanwhile, cook the tagliatelle in a large pan of salted boiling water for 2–3 minutes, until tender but still firm to the bite. Alternatively, cook according to the packet instructions.

Drain the pasta, add it to the pan with the lardons and garlic and toss well. Add the basil, season with sea salt and serve.

A piggy party

Pork fillet with cider vinegar on a bed of sweet potatoes

PREPARATION TIME: 20 MINUTES
COOKING TIME: 1½ HOURS

SERVES 6

6 tablespoons olive oil
1 kg (2¼ lb) pork fillet
1 aubergine, cut into large cubes
2 tomatoes, cut into large cubes
2 courgettes, cut into large cubes
2 garlic cloves, chopped
2 onions, chopped
200 ml (7 fl oz) dry cider
50 g (2 oz) unsalted butter, cut into pieces
600 g (1 lb 5 oz) sweet potatoes
150 ml (¼ pint) cider vinegar
2 tablespoons sugar
fresh flat-leaf parsley and fresh coriander leaves, to garnish

Preheat the oven to 160°C (325°F/Gas Mark 3). Heat the olive oil in a large, flameproof casserole. Add the pork and cook over a high heat, turning occasionally, for about 10 minutes, until evenly browned.

Lower the heat, add the aubergine, tomatoes, courgettes, garlic and onions and cook, stirring occasionally, for 5 minutes. Pour in the cider and bring to the boil. Cover and cook in the oven for 1 hour. Add the butter, return the casserole to the oven and cook for a further 15 minutes.

Meanwhile, cook the sweet potatoes in salted boiling water for about 20 minutes, until tender. Drain and mash coarsely with a fork. Keep warm.

Mix together the cider vinegar and sugar in a pan. Cook over a low heat, stirring until the sugar has dissolved, then continue to cook until reduced and syrupy.

Make a bed of sweet potato on each of six serving plates. Slice the pork. Divide the meat and vegetables, with their cooking juices, among the plates. Spoon a little vinegar syrup over each serving and garnish with parsley and coriander leaves.

A piggy party

Wild boar

Wild boar terrine

PREPARATION TIME: 45 MINUTES
MARINATING TIME: 4 HOURS
COOKING TIME: 3 HOURS

MAKES 3 × 500 g (1 lb 2 oz) JARS

600 g (1 lb 5 oz) boneless shoulder of wild boar
100 g (3½ oz) lardons, cut into thin batons
50 ml (2 fl oz) red port
100 ml (3½ fl oz) red wine
2 tablespoons Armagnac
8 juniper berries, crushed
1 teaspoon ground mixed spice
300 g (11 oz) pork belly
400 g (14 oz) pork blade
150 g (5 oz) pig's liver
2 shallots, chopped
2 garlic cloves, chopped
1 tablespoon salt
1 teaspoon fresh thyme
pepper

Cut 200 g (7 oz) of the wild boar into small cubes and place in a dish. Add the lardons, port, red wine, Armagnac, juniper berries and spice, mix well and leave to marinate for 4 hours.

Coarsely mince the remaining wild boar, the pork belly, pork blade and liver. Mix together the minced meat, shallots, garlic, salt, thyme and a pinch of pepper in a large bowl. Add the cubed wild boar, together with the marinade, and mix well.

Sterilize three preserving jars and their lids. Fill the jars with the terrine mixture, pressing it down well, and seal. Place the jars in a pan, add water to cover, place a weight on top of the jars to keep them submerged and simmer for 3 hours.

Remove the jars from the pan and leave to cool, then store in a dry place for several days before serving.

Marcassin pâté

PREPARATION TIME: 45 MINUTES
MARINATING: 24 HOURS
COOKING TIME: 2 HOURS

MAKES 1.5 kg (3¼ lb)

1 kg (2¼ lb) boneless shoulder of
  marcassin (wild boar under the age of 6 months)
100 g (3½ oz) smoked pork belly
2 onions
4 cloves
500 ml (18 fl oz) Côtes du Rhône or Shiraz wine
2 carrots, diced
3 bay leaves
1 fresh thyme sprig
400 g (14 oz) pork blade

4 teaspoons salt
25 g (1 oz) unsalted butter
4 shallots, thinly sliced
4 garlic cloves, thinly sliced
1 tablespoon cornflour
200 ml (7 fl oz) double cream
4 eggs, lightly beaten
3 tablespoons dark rum
pork fat or lard, for greasing

Cut half the wild boar and all the smoked pork belly into thin strips and place in a dish. Stud the onions with the cloves, add to the dish with the red wine, carrots, bay leaves and thyme and leave to marinate for 24 hours.

Preheat the oven to 120°C (250°F/Gas Mark ½). Coarsely mince the remaining wild boar and the pork blade, mix together in a bowl and add the salt. Melt the butter in a frying pan. Add the shallots and garlic and cook over a low heat, stirring occasionally, for 5 minutes, until softened. Stir the shallots and garlic into the meat mixture.

Remove the bay leaves and thyme from the marinade and reserve. Remove the strips of meat with a slotted spoon and add to the minced meat mixture. Mix together the cornflour and cream and add to the meat mixture with the eggs and rum. Mix well.

Grease a terrine with pork fat or lard and fill with the meat mixture, pressing down well. Arrange the bay leaves and thyme on top and place in a roasting tin. Pour boiling water into the tin to come about halfway up the sides of the terrine and cook in the oven for 1 hour, then cover with a lid and cook for 1 hour more.

Remove the terrine from the roasting tin and leave to cool, then store in a cool place for 24 hours before serving.

Dried fruit terrine

PREPARATION TIME: 45 MINUTES
COOKING TIME: 2¼ HOURS

MAKES 1 kg (3¼ lb)

20 g (¾ oz) unsalted butter
4 onions, sliced
1 kg (2¼ lb) boneless shoulder of wild boar
200 g (7 oz) pork fat
500 g (1 lb 2 oz) pork belly
4 teaspoons salt
a pinch of mild red chilli powder
a pinch of ground cinnamon
100 ml (3½ fl oz) white port
3 tablespoons plum brandy
100 ml (3½ fl oz) double cream
3 tablespoons chopped hazelnuts
3 tablespoons chopped pistachio nuts
3 tablespoons chopped almonds
5 prunes, stoned and chopped
5 dried apricots, stoned and chopped
1 fresh thyme sprig
1 fresh rosemary sprig

Preheat the oven to 120°C (250°/Gas Mark ½). Melt the butter in a frying pan. Add the onions and cook over a low heat, stirring occasionally, for about 8 minutes until softened and lightly coloured.

Cut 200 g (7 oz) of the wild boar and the pork fat into cubes. Coarsely mince the remaining meat. Mix together all the ingredients, except the herbs, in a large bowl.

Spoon the mixture into a terrine, pressing down well, and top with the thyme and rosemary. Place the terrine in a roasting tin. Pour boiling water into the tin to come about halfway up the sides of the terrine. Cook in the oven for 2 hours.

Remove the terrine from the roasting tin and leave to cool, then store in a cool place for 24 hours before serving.

`Back from the hunt' wild boar casserole

PREPARATION TIME: 20 MINUTES
COOKING TIME: 2 HOURS

SERVES 6

4 tablespoons olive oil
1 kg (2¼ lb) boneless shoulder of wild boar, cut into 5 cm (2 inch) cubes
2 onions, sliced
1 tablespoon plain flour
1 litre (1¾ pints) Côtes du Rhône or Shiraz wine
2 garlic cloves
3 shallots, halved
1 teaspoon ground mixed spice
1 tablespoon beef stock powder
70 g (2¾ oz) unsalted butter
500 g (1 lb 2 oz) porcini mushrooms
300 g (11 oz) chanterelle mushrooms
300 g (11 oz) cooked chestnuts

Heat the olive oil in a large, flameproof casserole. Add the wild boar and onions and cook over a medium heat, stirring frequently, for about 10 minutes, until evenly browned. Stir in the flour and cook, stirring constantly, for 2–4 minutes, until golden. Stir in the red wine and add the garlic, shallots and mixed spice.

Mix the stock powder with 500 ml (18 fl oz) boiling water in a jug, add to the casserole and bring back to the boil. Lower the heat and simmer for 1½ hours, until the meat is very tender.

Remove the meat with a slotted spoon and keep warm. Bring the cooking liquid back to the boil and cook until reduced and syrupy. Beat in 50 g (2 oz) of the butter.

Meanwhile, melt the remaining butter in a non-stick pan. Add both types of mushrooms and the chestnuts and cook over a high heat, stirring occasionally, for about 5 minutes.

Place the wild boar in a warm dish, add the mushrooms and chestnuts and pour the sauce over them. Serve immediately.

Jugged wild boar with spelt and saffron risotto

PREPARATION TIME: 45 MINUTES
COOKING TIME: 1¾ HOURS

SERVES 6

1 kg (2¼ lb) boneless shoulder of wild boar,
  cut into 5 cm (2 inch) cubes
100 g (3½ oz) lardons
1 litre (1¾ pints) Côtes du Rhône or Shiraz wine
2 shallots, sliced
3 garlic cloves, sliced
2 bay leaves
1 leek, sliced
1 bouquet garni
1 tablespoon beef stock powder
400 g (14 oz) spelt wheat
2 onions, sliced
50 g (2 oz) unsalted butter
200 ml (7 fl oz) double cream
a pinch of saffron threads
50 g (2 oz) Parmesan cheese, grated

Put the wild boar and lardons into a large, flameproof casserole and cook over a medium heat, stirring frequently, until evenly browned. Add the red wine, shallots, garlic, bay leaves, leek and bouquet garni. Mix the stock powder with 500 ml (18 fl oz) boiling water in a jug, add it to the casserole and bring to the boil. Lower the heat and simmer for 1½ hours, until the meat is very tender.

Meanwhile, put the spelt wheat and onions into a saucepan, add water to cover and bring to the boil. Lower the heat and simmer for 45 minutes, adding more boiling water if necessary.

When the meat is tender, remove it from the casserole with a slotted spoon and keep warm. Remove and discard the bay leaves and bouquet garni. Bring the cooking liquid back to the boil and cook until reduced and syrupy. Beat in the butter.

When the spelt wheat is tender, cook until the water has evaporated, then stir in the cream and saffron. Cook over a low heat for 5 minutes, then stir in the Parmesan. Arrange the wild boar in a serving bowl with the risotto in the centre. Spoon the sauce over them and serve.

Wild boar fillet with Muscatel butter

PREPARATION TIME: 30 MINUTES
COOKING TIME: 20 MINUTES

SERVES 6

3 black radishes, thinly sliced into rounds
50 g (2 oz) unsalted butter
1 teaspoon sugar
4 tablespoons olive oil
1 kg (2¼ lb) fillet of wild boar
1 kg (2¼ lb) seedless white grapes, halved
175 ml (6 fl oz) Muscatel, white port or Sauternes wine

Put the radishes in a saucepan, add water to cover, 10 g (¼ oz) of the butter and the sugar and bring to the boil. Lower the heat and simmer until the water has completely evaporated and the radishes are glazed.

Heat the olive oil in a frying pan. Add the wild boar and cook over a high heat, turning occasionally, for about 10 minutes, until evenly browned and cooked through. Remove from the pan and keep warm.

Add the grapes to the pan, lower the heat and cook for 2 minutes, then stir in the wine, scraping up any sediment from the base of the pan with a wooden spoon. Beat in the remaining butter.

Slice the fillet into thin strips and arrange randomly on individual plates with the radishes and grapes. Spoon the sauce over them and serve.

wild boar chops with tart red fruits

PREPARATION TIME: 10 MINUTES
COOKING TIME: 20 MINUTES

SERVES 6

3 Cox's Orange Pippins or other small eating apples
25 g (1 oz) unsalted butter
6 wild boar chops
4 teaspoons brandy
200 ml (7 fl oz) Côtes du Rhône or Shiraz wine
50 ml (2 fl oz) crème de cassis
50 g (2 oz) gooseberries
50 g (2 oz) dewberries or blackberries
50 g (2 oz) raspberries

Peel, core and quarter the apples. Melt the butter in a frying pan. Add the apple quarters
and cook, turning occasionally, for about 5 minutes, until golden brown. Remove from the pan
and reserve the cooking juices.

Add the chops to the pan and cook for 5 minutes on each side, then remove from the pan
and keep warm.

Add the brandy to the pan, heat for a few seconds and ignite. When the flames have died down,
stir in the red wine, scraping up any sediment from the base with a wooden spoon. Add the
crème de cassis and cook until reduced.

Beat the reserved cooking juices into the sauce, add the fruit and cook for 1 minute. Divide the
chops and apples among individual serving plates and spoon the sauce over them.

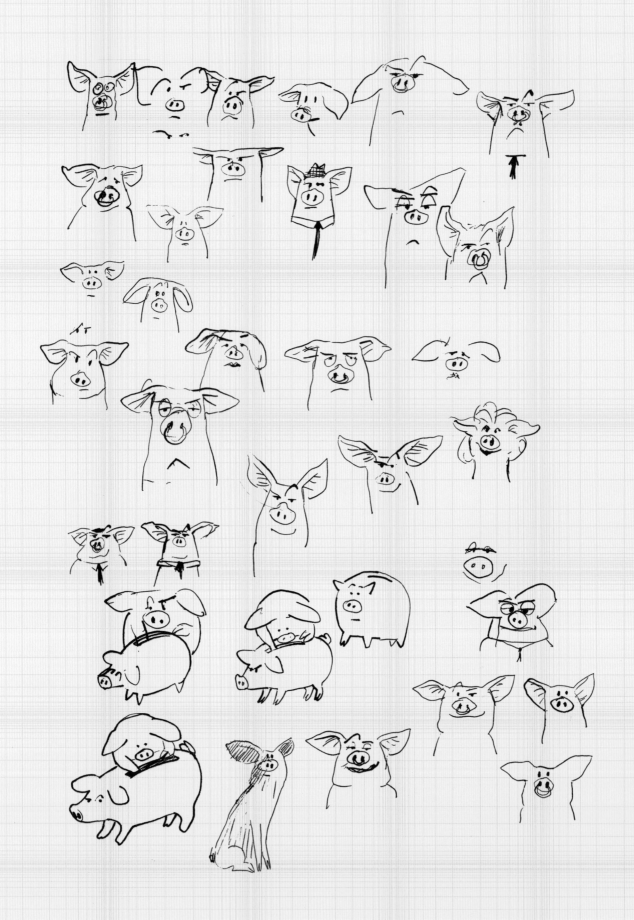

Index

TABLE OF RECIPES

Index

INDEX

CHEESES AND WINES

Cheese

Appenzeller (page 116)
Appenzeller is a semi-hard cow's milk cheese made in Switzerland. It tastes mild, and has a nutty or fruity flavour thanks to a herbal and wine brine that is applied to the cheese while it is curing.

Comté (pages 122, 136, 328)
Comté is a semi-hard unpasteurised cow's milk cheese made in France. It is salty and has a mild nutty flavour when young, but becomes more complex and varied with age. It is a good melting cheese.

Gruyère (pages 122, 136, 138, 328)
Gruyère is a hard unpasteurised cow's milk cheese made in Switzerland. It has a creamy (when young), nutty, earthy flavour. It is considered a good cooking cheese because it melts well and has a flavour that doesn't overpower other ingredients.

Emmental (page 128)
Emmental is a medium-hard cow's milk cheese made in Switzerland. It has large holes and a nutty flavour, and is often used in sandwiches.

Fourme d'Ambert (page 134)
Fourme d'Ambert is a soft creamy pasteurised cow's milk cheese made in France. It has a mild light blue vein through it, and a savoury, nutty flavour.

Saint-Marcellin (page 328)
Saint-Marcellin is a soft creamy unpasteurised cheese made from cow's or goat's milk. It tastes slightly yeasty and has a very rustic nutty flavour.

Saint-Moret (page 116)
Saint-Moret is a cream cheese made in France.

Sarrassou (page 236)
Sarrassou is a white French cheese best described as half way between cottage cheese and yoghurt.

Wine

Beaujolais (page 156)
Beaujolais is a historical wine-producing region in France, just north of Lyon. Wines from Beaujolais are primarily red and are made from the Gamay grape. They are traditionally light, fruity, dry wines that can be drunk early.

Bourgogne Aligoté (page 162)
Aligoté is a white grape grown in and around the Burgundy region of France. Wines made in Burgundy from this grape are labelled as being from the official wine-making area Bourgogne Aligoté AC. They are citrusy and nutty in flavour.

Chardonnay (page 162)
The Chardonnay grape is versatile and easy to grow, and is harvested all around the world. As a result, these white wines vary greatly in flavour, but they are often soft and fruity when young and develop vanilla and caramel flavours as they age.

Côtes du Rhône (pages 232, 250, 260, 344, 348, 350, 354)
The Côtes du Rhône AC is one of the official wine-making areas within the wider Rhône region of France and includes vineyards in both the north and the south. Most Côtes du Rhône wines are red and are made from Grenach Noir, Shiraz (Syrah), Carignan, Counoise and Mourvedre grapes. Traditionally quite heavy wines, Côte du Rhône reds have recently become lighter and fruitier.

Mâcon (page 82)
Mâcon wines come from the Mâconnais part of Burgundy, France. They are light wines that should be drunk early. The red wines are predominantly made from Gamay Noir and Pinot Noir grapes, and the white wines come from Pinot Blanc and Chardonnay grapes.

Muscatel (pages 168, 84, 352)
Is a sweet fortified dessert wine made from the muscat species of grapes, which are grown all around the world.

Riesling (pages 240, 242, 324)
Riesling is a type of white grape grown historically in France, Germany and Italy. Wines made from Riesling grapes have a spicy, fruity flavour and range from dry to sweet.

Saint Joseph (page 276)
Saint Joseph is an area in the Rhône region of France that produces mostly red wines. These are predominantly made from Shiraz (Syrah) grapes, and are considered by the locals to be resemble Beaujolais.

Shiraz (pages 232, 250, 260, 276, 344, 348, 350, 354)
Shiraz, otherwise known as Syrah, is a high-quality grape that is used to make red wine. Almost always full-bodied, the flavour of Shiraz wines does vary, but young Shiraz wines are generally rich in colour, with strong spice and pepper flavours. As they mature they become more earthy and develop flavours of sweet blackberries, black currants and plums. Shiraz wines can often be a blend of more than one grape type.

Vin jaune (page 258)
Vin jaune is a white wine made in the Jura region of France from late-harvest Savagnin grapes. During production, the wine undergoes a process similar to that when making sherry, and the result is a sherry-like, delicate, nutty wine that ages extremely well and can be matured for decades.

SOURCES: PIGGY PEOPLE WE LIKE...

FRANCE

Teyssier Verdun
Place de Verdun
07320 Saint Agrève
Tel. 04 75 30 14 22

Salaison Pichon
Le Bourg
43290 Raucoules
Tel. 04 71 59 92 76

Les produits d'Auvergne chez Teil
6 rue de Lappe
75011 Paris
Tel. 01 47 00 41 28

C.C.A. La Charcuterie Alsacienne
196 rue de Vaugirard
75015 Paris
Tel. 01 45 66 87 38

Charcuterie Sibilia
102 cours Lafayette
69003 Lyon
Tel. 04 78 62 36 28

Charcuterie Bonnard
36 rue Grenette
69002 Lyon
Tel. 04 78 42 19 63

Gast
102 cours Lafayette
69003 Lyon
Tel. 04 78 62 32 25

Andouillette Duval
171 rue de la Convention
75015 Paris
Tel. 01 45 30 14 08

Andouilles Rivalan Quidu
5 rue de Bellevue
56160 Guéméné sur Scorff
Tel. 02 97 51 21 10

Andouillerie de la vallée de la Sienne
Les Planches
50450 Saint Denis le Gast
Tel. 02 33 61 44 20

Treo
112 rue des Dames
75017 Paris
Tel. 01 44 69 94 03

Jabugo Iberico & co
11 rue Clément Marot
75008 Paris
Tel. 01 47 20 03 13

Bellota-Bellota
18 rue Jean Nicot
75007 Paris
Tel. 01 53 59 96 96

S.E.E. Pléchot
11 rue Maréchal Foch
65500 Vic en Bigorre
Tel. 05 62 96 86 72

Salaisons Pyrénéennes
2 rue Anatole France
65320 Borderes sur l'Echez
Tel. 05 62 37 00 01

Pierre Oteiza
Route d'Urepel
64430 Aldudes
Tel. 05 59 37 56 11

Montauzer
Quartier Bourgade
64520 Guiche
Tel. 05 59 56 84 04

Jean-Philippe Darrieumerlou
43 rue Carnot
40800 Aire sur l'Adour
Tel. 05 58 71 77 28

De Louche à Taie
4, place Souvenir
33125 Louchats
Tel. 05 56 88 51 40

Charcuterie Blaise
28 rue du Général-de-Gaulle
29590 Le Faou
Tel. 02 98 81 91 51

Charcuterie Besançon
1 rue Fret
29160 Lanvéoc
Tel. 02 98 27 50 54

Charcuterie Léon
10 rue Saint Yves
29290 Saint Renan
Tel. 02 98 84 21 47

Pierre Schmidt
36 Grand'rue
67000 Strasbourg
Tel. 03 88 32 39 63

Porcus
6 place Temple Neuf
67000 Strasbourg
Tel. 03 88 23 19 38

Tempé Gustave & fils
68 route de Soultz
68200 Mulhouse
Tel. 03 89 52 32 33

Bouheret
26 rue Fauche
25500 Morteau
Tel. 03 81 67 10 39

**Decreuse Salaison
du Haut Doubs**
Lieu-dit La Cluse
25300 La Cluse et Mijoux
Tel. 03 81 69 55 00

*For those who live
near the spanish border:*

Chez Peïo
Dantxaria

Charcuterias y embutidos
'El Sedentario'
Camping/dancing El Faro
Hondarribia Guipuzcoa (Fontarabie)

UNITED KINGDOM AND AUSTRALIA

NORTHERN IRELAND

Ballylagan Organic Farm Shop
12 Ballylagan Road
Straid Ballyclare
Co Antrim
Tel. 028 9332 2867

Organic pioneer stocking home-reared beef, lamb, pork, poultry and eggs.

ENGLAND

The North

C Nicholson & Son
140 Park View
Whitley Bay
Tyne and Wear
NE26 3QN
Tel. 0191 252 5250

For popular fine sausages, including varieties such as pork and ale, and lamb and apricot.

Higginsons Ltd
Keswick House
Main Street
Grange Over Sands
Cumbria
LA11 6AB

For black pudding.

Paul Flintoft Traditional Family Butchers
12 High Street
Kippax
North Yorkshire
LS25 7AB
Tel. 0113 287 2482
www.paulflintoft.co.uk

For 17 different types of sausage.

Pugh Piglet's
Bowgreave House Farm
Bowgreave
Garstang
Preston
Lancashire
PR3 1YE
Tel. 020 8221 3939
www.pughspiglets.co.uk

Mail order service available.

Scotts of York Butchers
81 Low Petergate
York
YO1

For York ham.

Sillfield Farm
Peter Gott
Endmoor
Kendal, Cumbria
LA8 0HZ
enquire@sillfield.co.uk

For wild boar and Cumberland sausages.

Steve Lewis Butchers
152 Greasby Road
Greasby
Wirral
Liverpool
CH49 3NQ
Tel. 0151 678 7990

For popular low-fat, low-salt black pudding.

East Anglia

The Denham Estate
Denham, Barrow
Bury St Edmunds
Suffolk
IP29 5EQ
Tel. 0128 481 0231

For a range of traditional British livestock breeds of beef, pork and lamb.

Viking Sausages
Tel. 0167 383 8205
www.vikingsausages.co.uk

For sausages handmade to a recipe dating back to the 1860s. Mail order available.

Midlands

Home farm of Pytchley
Butchers Lane
Pytchley
Kettering
Northamptonshire
NN14 1EJ
Tel. 0153 679 1840
www.homefarmofpytchley.co.uk

For Middle White pork.

Huntsman Farm
Richard Vaughn
Goodrich
Ross on Wye
Herefordshire
HR9 6JN

For rare breed pork.

Rightons Of Shipston
16 Sheep Street
Shipston-on-Stour
Warwickshire
CV36 4AF
Tel. 0160 866 1445

South West

Heritage Prime
Shedbush Farm
Muddyford Lane
Stanton St Gabriel
Bridport
Dorset
DT6 6OR
Tel. 0129 748 9304

Well Hung Meat Co.
Tordean Farm
Dean Prior
Buckfastleigh
Devon
Tel. 0845 230 3131

For mail-order organic meat, including the popular seasonal meat box (reared sustainably and naturally in Devon and Cornwall).

South East

Laverstoke Park Butchers Shop
Southley Farm
Overton
Basingstoke
Hampshire
RG25 3DR
Tel. 0125 677 1571
www.laverstokepork.co.uk

Richard Guy's Real Meat Co.
Tel. 01985 840562
www.realmeat.co.uk

London

Borough Market
8 Southwark Street
London
SE1 1TL
Tel. 020 7407 1002

The Wild Boar Stall (Peter Gott) for rare breed pork, wild boar, sausage and hams: most Fridays and Saturdays.

The Ginger Pig
8–10 Moxon Street
Marylebone
W1U 4EW
Tel. 020 7935 7788

H G Walter
51 Palliser Road
Hammersmith
W14 9EB
Tel. 020 7385 6466

Lidgate
110 Holland Park Avenue
W11 4UA
Tel. 020 7727 8243

M. Moen & Sons
24 The Pavement
Clapham
SW4 0JA
Tel. 020 7622 1624

Randalls
113 Wandsworth Bridge Road
Fulham
SW6 2TE
Tel. 020 7736 3426

Villandry
170 Great Portland Street
London
W1W 5QB
Tel. 020 7631 3131

SCOTLAND

Ballencreiff Rare Pedigree Pigs
Farm Shop
Ballencreiff Gardens
Longniddry
East Lothian
EH32 0PJ
Tel. 0187 587 0551

Blackmount Organics
8 The Wynd
Biggar
Lanarkshire
ML12 6BU
Tel. 0189 922 1747
www.blackmountfoods.com

Findlays the Butcher
116 Portobello High Street
Edinburgh
EH15 1AL
Tel. 0131 669 2783
www.findlayofportobello.co.uk

Puddledub Pork & Fifeshire Bacon Co.Ltd
Clentre Farmhouse
Auchtertool
Kirkcaldy
Fife
KY2 5XG
Tel. 0159 278 0246
www.puddledub.co.uk

WALES

Carter's Family Butchers
King St
Ludlow
Shropshire
SY8 1AQ
Tel. 0158 487 4665

For home-made sausages.

Pembrokeshire Pork & Sausages
Dolwerdd Farm
Boncath
Dyfed
SA37 0JW
Tel. 0123 984 1268

AUSTRALIA

New South Wales

AC Butchery
174 Marion Street
Leichardt, Sydney, 2040
Tel. 02 9569 8687

Cliff Penny's Quality Butcher
18 Bungan Street
Mona Vale
Tel. 02 9997 1581

Pino's Butchery
45 President Avenue
Kogarah, Sydney, 2217
Tel. 02 9587 4818

The Sweet Bangalow Pork Company
PO Box 1220
Ballina, 2478
Tel. 02 6681 3800
www.sweetpork.com.au

Terry Wright's Gourmet Meats
32 Clovelly Road
Randwick, Sydney, 2031
Tel. 02 9398 1038

TJ's Quality Meats
319 Darling Street
Balmain, Sydney, 2041
Tel. 02 9810 2911

Queensland

Black Pearl Epicure
36 Baxter Street
Fortitude Valley, Brisbane, 4006
Tel. 08 3257 2144

Farmers Market
Brisbane Powerhouse
Lamington Street
New Farm, Brisbane, 4005

South Australia

Adelaide Central Market
Gouger Street
Adelaide, 5000

Barossa Fine Foods
Shop 60, Central Market
Gouger Street
Adelaide, 5000
Tel. 08 8231 2575

Bottega Rotolo
7 Osmond Terrace
Norwood, Adelaide, 5067
Tel. 08 8362 0455

Schulz Butchers
42 Murray Street
Angaston, 5353
Tel. 08 8564 2145

Tasmania

Bayside Meats
628 Sandy Bay Road
Sandy Bay, 7006
Tel. 03 6225 1482

Wursthaus Kitchen
1 Montpelier Retreat
Hobart, 7000
Tel. 03 6224 0644

Victoria

Enoteca Sileno
21 Amess Street
North Carlton, Melbourne, 3054
Melbourne
Tel. 03 9347 5044

Hagen's Organic Meats
Stall 16, Queen Victoria Market
corner Elizabeth and Victoria streets
Melbourne, 3000
Tel. 03 9329 5534

Peter Bouchier Butcher
551 Malvern Road
Toorak, Melbourne, 3142
Tel. 03 9827 3629

Queen Victoria Market
corner Elizabeth and Victoria streets
Melbourne, 3000

South Melbourne Market
corner Cecil and Coventry streets
South Melbourne 3205
Tel. 03 9209 6295,

Western Australia

Mondo Butchers
824 Beaufort Street
Inglewood, Perth, 6052
Tel. 08 9371 6350

Author's acknowledgements

For my shepherdess and my little chickens, Jean, Zoé, Basile

With many thanks to Nicoco for putting up with me.

Thanks to my whole team for letting me hog their attention morning, noon and night.

Thanks to Marie-Pierre for her talent with the camera, to José for reviving the pig, to Emanuel and his dream team for their confidence in me.

Thanks to Saint-Agrève for my healthy red cheeks...

A note about the book

Many of the recipes in this book contain raw egg, soft unpasteurised cheese, or uncooked and processed meats. These foods may have health implications for the very young, elderly or ill, or for pregnant women. Please read the recipes carefully and if in doubt contact your doctor for advice.

Phaidon Press Limited
Regent's Wharf
All Saints Street
London N1 9PA

www.phaidon.com

First published in English 2007
© 2007 Phaidon Press Limited

ISBN 978 0 7148 4761 0 (UK edition)

First published in French by Marabout (Hachette Livre) as *Cochon & Fils*.
© 2005 Marabout (Hachette Livre)

A CIP catalogue record for this book is available from the British Library.

Hand-written titles: *Carlotta*

English edition layouts by Sandra Zellmer

Printed in China